THE GOSPEL 33 AD

PAUL LEHR

Copyright © 2019 Paul Lehr

All rights reserved

If you would like to share this book with another person, please purchase an additional copy for each recipient. If you are reading this book and did not purchase it, or it was not purchased for your use only, then please return to your favorite ebook retailer and purchase your own copy.

Book layout by www.ebooklaunch.com

Contents

Utmost Importance 1

Chapter 1: Simple Legal Argument 4

Chapter 2: Court in Session 8

Chapter 3: Jesus Christ 13

Chapter 4: Resurrection 19

Chapter 5: Spring Feasts 25

Chapter 6: Fullness of Time 35

Chapter 7: Passion Week 45

Chapter 8: Listen Up!!! 62

About the Author 87

Utmost Importance

This is the most important decision a person will ever make. Eternal destiny is on the line and at stake. The idea bears repeating. God takes the time in Scripture to repeat Himself numerous times. This is the good news of Jesus Christ.

But what is of the utmost importance is stated by the Apostle Paul. This is the priority. As believers in Jesus Christ we should draw a line in the sand and stick a flag in the ground over this issue. If a person does not get the issue of the gospel of Jesus Christ right, big time eternal problems.

1 Corinthians 15:1-4 Now, brothers, I want to remind you of the gospel I preached to you, which you received and on which you have taken your stand by which also you are saved, if you hold fast the word which I preached to you, unless you believed in vain. *For I delivered to you as of first importance* **what I also received, that Christ died for our sins according to the Scriptures, and that He was buried, and that He was raised on the third day according to the Scriptures...**

Jesus Christ died. He was buried. And He was raised.

This is the gospel message of Jesus Christ. The gospel is the **ευαγγελιον/euaggelion.** This is really "good news".

Here is how Strong's Concordance defines "gospel". It is the glad tidings of salvation through Christ. This is the proclamation of the grace of God manifest and pledged in Christ. As the messianic rank of Jesus was proved by his words, his deeds, and his death, the narrative of the sayings, deeds, and death of Jesus Christ came to be called the gospel or glad tidings.

The resume of Christ is sequentially ordered in Strong's definition of the gospel. The glad tidings of the kingdom of God soon to be set up, subsequently also of Jesus the Messiah, the founder of this kingdom. After the death of Christ, the term comprises also the preaching of (concerning) Jesus Christ as having suffered death on the cross to procure eternal salvation for the men in the kingdom of God, but as restored to life and exalted to the right hand of God in heaven, thence to return in majesty to consummate the kingdom of God.

The issue of the gospel is not an intellectual decision. The gospel is a moral issue. Does God exist and does He take the issue of sin seriously? If so, then there is accountability. The issue needs serious attention. Eternal life and eternal death are on the line. The destination of your eternal soul is at stake. This is about getting your heart, soul, and mind right with the Creator.

This good news is for everybody! God does not discriminate. The most brutal, unsavory character can be saved from eternal hell if they believe the gospel message. One can think up the vilest person in their mind and that person too can be saved with their belief in Jesus Christ.

There is no sliding scale or grade curve when it comes to sin. To quote a pastor I know, "We are all equal at the foot of the cross."

Even a barbaric Scythian can be saved by the cross work of Jesus...

Colossians 3:11 *a renewal* **in which there is no** *distinction between* **Greek and Jew, circumcised and uncircumcised, barbarian, Scythian, slave and freeman, but Christ is all, and in all.**

Jesus Christ knew His destiny before the creation of the world. His death on the cross was planned before the Earth was formed. The three verses below will hurt your head when you stop and think about them.

Revelation 13:8 All who dwell on the earth will worship him, *everyone* **whose name has not been written from the foundation of the world in the book of life of the Lamb who has been slain.**

1 Peter 1:20a For He was foreknown before the foundation of the world...

2 Timothy 1:9 He has saved us and called us with a holy calling, not because of our own works, but by His own purpose and by the grace He granted us in Christ Jesus before time eternal.

Believers in Christ were chosen before the world was made. This does not mean we do not have free will. God is a gentleman. He does not force Himself on us. God does not want a robot. He wants our heart and free choice. He wants to be chosen. The first four commandments of the Ten Commandments imply we have a choice whether we worship God or not. A consequence is stated but God does not make us do anything. He knows what we are going to do and the choices we will make. He gives us that freedom.

Ephesians 1:4 just as He chose us in Him before the foundation of the world, that we would be holy and blameless before Him. In love...

God knows all and He is across the scope of time. He has always known us even before our lives on earth start. He even knows how long we are going to live. He has it covered.

Jeremiah 1:5 "Before I formed you in the womb I knew you, and before you were born I consecrated you; I have appointed you a prophet to the nations."

Psalm 139:14-16 I will give thanks to You, for I am fearfully and wonderfully made; wonderful are Your works, and my soul knows it very well. My frame was not hidden from You, when I was made in secret, and skillfully wrought in the depths of the earth; Your eyes have seen my unformed substance; and in Your book were all written the days that were ordained for me, when as yet there was not one of them.

Chapter 1

Simple Legal Argument

At the core of the need for the gospel message is a simple legal argument and matter. God made this very clear from the beginning of time in the Garden of Eden. Listen and obey God's directions. "Eat all you want except for one." There are consequences. Some consequences are good and some are bad.

Genesis 2:16-17 The Lord God commanded the man, saying, "From any tree of the garden you may eat freely; but from the tree of the knowledge of good and evil you shall not eat, for in the day that you eat from it <u>you will surely die</u>."

As time progressed, Moses was given the Law for the nation of Israel on Mount Sinai. God communicated His Law to Moses approximately 3,600 years ago. These directions were given to Moses approximately 1,600 years before Christ. In total, there were 613 laws given. This number includes the Ten Commandments. Jews have even broken down the number of negative and positive commands. 365 are negative commands and 248 are positive commands. Read the first five books (**Genesis, Exodus, Leviticus, Numbers,** and **Deuteronomy**) of the Bible for these laws or mitzvoth (Hebrew term).

As far as God is concerned, there is no separation of moral and legal code. Culturally and legally the United States is different. We have a separation of church and state. That is not the intended case with God and His nation Israel.

Well so what if we break God's Law? What is the big deal? Sin is a big deal to God. It does not matter the offense. If you break the law, the punishment is death. It does not matter if one steals, lies, commits murder or adultery, covets, or whatever. There are no "shades of grey" when it comes to sin. There is not a sliding scale for sin. One sin is not more condemning than another. If you break one, you break them all. That is God's standard.

James 2:10 For whoever keeps the whole law and yet stumbles in one point, he has become guilty of all.

Romans 6:23a For the wages of sin is death...

1 Corinthians 15:56 The sting of death is sin, and the power of sin is the law...

The critic often says, "Well, the Ten Commandments are in the Old Testament and we live during the church age in the New Testament. Jesus took care of the Law."

A message for the critic, the Mosaic Law is still present whether you believe it or not. The issue is whether or not you have Jesus to cover your mess. The Mosaic Law and the Ten Commandments have not gone away. Jesus Himself made this very clear.

Matthew 5:17 "Do not think that I have come to abolish the Law or the Prophets; I have not come to abolish them but to fulfill them."

If we are at all honest with ourselves, we have some serious issues. The Mosaic Law has incredible standards. Who are we kidding! In our current state of humanity, we are all guilty. Adam introduced sin to humanity. The result was bodily death.

Romans 5:12 Therefore, just as through one man sin entered into the world, and death through sin, and so death spread to all men, because all sinned...

1 Corinthians 15:22 For as in Adam all die, so also in Christ all will be made alive.

Sin is the reason for illness and death. We don't know when or how we are going to die. But we do know the reason for death, sin. Missing the mark or missing the moral standard is the reason we sweat for crying out loud. Weeds were not supposed to grow. A rose was not intended to have thorns. We were not originally created for hard labor.

So, the next time somebody asks, "Why does God allows bad things to happen? How could a loving God let that horrible thing occur?"

We need to take a long, hard look in the mirror and get really honest. Sin is why bad and evil things happen in the world.

Genesis 3:17-19 Then to Adam He said, "Because you have listened to the voice of your wife, and have eaten from the tree about which I commanded you, saying, 'You shall not eat from it'; cursed is the ground because of you; in toil you will eat of it all the days of your life. Both thorns and thistles it shall grow for you; and you will eat the plants of the field; by the sweat of your face you will eat bread, till you return to the ground, because from it you were taken; for you are dust, and to dust you shall return."

As individuals, it is not our place to judge others regardless of their actions. Every person on the planet has a lifestyle or mental attitude issue that can be taken to task. There is no sliding scale or grading on the curve when it comes to sin. "Well my sin is not as bad as…" Nonsense, judgment belongs to God.

James 4:12 There is *only* one Lawgiver and Judge, the One who is able to save and to destroy; but who are you who judge your neighbor?

We are all in need of sin remission. Every single one of us is a sinner. We all have sin in our lives.

Ecclesiastes 7:20 Indeed, there is not a righteous man on earth who continually does good and who never sins.

Romans 3:23 for all have sinned and fall short of the glory of God…

We all (except a group of believers at the rapture) have a set time and date with the grave. It does not matter what our bodies look like. One cannot diet, vitamin, or exercise their way from the Pit. It does not matter if you are rich or poor. One cannot buy their way out of Sheol.

Psalm 89:48 What man can live and not see death? Can he deliver his soul from the power of Sheol? Selah.

Psalm 49:14 As sheep they are appointed for Sheol; death shall be their shepherd; and the upright shall rule over them in the morning, and their form shall be for Sheol to consume so that they have no habitation.

Job 26:6 Naked is Sheol before Him, and Abaddon has no covering.

The meaning of Abaddon is "destruction". Sin is naked awareness before God. In the final analysis, there is no covering of sin apart from the cross work of Christ. God has always made provision for the sin of humanity. Apart from God, sin will be exposed, bare, and raw. Its path leads to destruction.

Proverbs 15:11 Sheol and Abaddon *lie open* before the LORD, How much more the hearts of men!

Death is knocking. The open throat and grave of death await.

Chapter 1 Study Guide

What is the consequence for breaking God's Law?

Do the Mosaic Law and the 10 Commandments still matter? Why?

How is the Law applied to the believer in Christ versus non-believers?

What is Christ's role in regards to the Law?

Chapter 2

Court in Session

All Rise... And you have entered the Eternal Heavenly court room. God the Father is presiding over the court.

You have died. So how do you plead? Innocent or guilty. It is a loaded question, you are dead. Satan is the prosecution. There is a defense attorney provided for you if you accept His counsel. The defense attorney provided is offering free services if you are accepting. He will defend you free of charge. He is at your service if you believe He can do the job.

Your life is on trial. You will be judged by your actions. It is stated twice in **Revelation 20**, you will be judged by your deeds. Be careful what you ask for. There is a written record.

Revelation 20:12-13 And I saw the dead, the great and the small, standing before the throne, and books were opened; and another book was opened, which is *the book* of life; and the dead were judged from the <u>things which were written in the books, according to their deeds</u>. And the sea gave up the dead which were in it, and death and Hades gave up the dead which were in them; and they were judged, <u>every one of them according to their deeds.</u>

Satan the Prosecutor

It is important to understand and know your prosecutor. His name is Satan. He has a significant history of pointing out the sins of humanity. As a prosecutor, he never rests.

Revelation 12:10 Then I heard a loud voice in heaven, saying, "Now the salvation, and the power, and the kingdom of our God and the authority of His Christ have come, for the accuser of our brethren has been thrown down, he who accuses them before our God day and night.

This is hardly a fair trial. We know Satan is a prosecuting attorney from multiple sources in the Bible in both the Old and New Testament. Granted, we are guilty. But he is a tattletale all of the time and a very effective prosecutor.

Zechariah 3:1 Then he showed me Joshua the high priest standing before the angel of the LORD, and Satan standing at his right hand to accuse him.

Some would ask the question. Who is in charge Satan or God? At times, God will allow Satan to test people with limits. God grants that authority to Satan with **Job**. Satan knows who is in charge. When God calls, Satan comes. See **Job 2** for a detailed account of a conversation with Satan and God.

Job 2:6 So the LORD said to Satan, "Behold, he is in your power, only spare his life."

God is still in charge.

Revelation 2:10b ...Behold, the devil is about to cast some of you into prison, so that you will be tested...

Satan is going to "test" and it is the Greek word **πειραζο/peirazo**. It is defined as: to test one maliciously, craftily to put to the proof his feelings or judgments; to try or test one's faith, virtue, character, by enticement to sin, tempt. - Strong's Concordance

When bad things happen, it may or may not be Satan. Job never knew the source of his angst. Sometimes it is us that is the source of our issues.

God the Father: Judge

God the Father is the presiding judge. He is absolutely holy and perfect in justice. There will be no plea bargain.

Psalm 89:14 <u>Righteousness and justice are the foundation of Your throne</u>; lovingkindness and truth go before You.

Psalm 97:2 Clouds and thick darkness surround Him; <u>righteousness and justice are the foundation of His throne.</u>

God cannot stand sin. He hates sin and His character demands that sin is punished, no exceptions.

Psalm 7:11 God is a righteous judge, and a God who has indignation every day.

Psalm 5:5 The boastful shall not stand before Your eyes; You hate all who do iniquity.

God cannot be bought or bribed. It does not matter how deep your pockets are. You don't have enough money or material possessions. Justice will be served.

Proverbs 11:4 <u>Riches do not profit</u> in the day of wrath, but righteousness delivers from death.

Zephaniah 1:18 <u>Neither their silver nor their gold will be able to deliver them</u> on the day of the LORD'S wrath; and all the earth will be devoured in the fire of His jealousy, for He will make a complete end, indeed a terrifying one, of all the inhabitants of the earth.

Community service is not an option. One cannot work away their crime and sentence. One cannot earn their way to God. Humanity is not going to work their way to Heaven.

Romans 3:28 For we maintain that a man is justified by faith <u>apart from works</u> of the Law.

2 Timothy 1:9 He has saved us and called us with a holy calling, <u>not because of our own works</u>, but by His own purpose and by the grace He granted us in Christ Jesus before time eternal.

Titus 3:5 He saved us, <u>not by the righteous deeds we had done</u>, but according to His mercy, through the washing of new birth and renewal by the Holy Spirit.

Ephesians 2:8-9 For by grace you have been saved through faith; and that not of yourselves, it is the gift of God; <u>not as a result of works</u>, so that no one may boast.

God the Father accepts only one payment for sin, the shedding of sinless blood on behalf of the guilty. Sinless blood is the currency of God. This concept of sinless blood covering sin starts back in the Garden of Eden. An animal or animals made in perfection during creation were sacrificed and skinned to allow for Adam and Eve to be clothed or covered. Clothing is a reminder of sin.

Genesis 3:21 The LORD God made garments of skin for Adam and his wife, and clothed them.

We were created naked and it was not a big deal. But, all of that changed when sin was introduced to the creation.

Genesis 2:25 And the man and his wife were both naked and were not ashamed.

Dollars, Pounds, Shekels, and precious metals do not count in God's economy. They are not acceptable currency.

1 Peter 1:18 ...knowing that you were not redeemed with perishable things like silver or gold from your futile way of life inherited from your forefathers...

There is no way any of us qualify for the standard of sinless blood. None of us are sinless. We are all guilty.

Romans 3:23 for all have sinned and fall short of the glory of God...

Chapter 2 Study Questions

In the presence of God in Heaven, how does Satan relate to believers in Christ and Israel?

Describe the characteristics of God the Father as a judge.

What currency does God the Father accept for sin?

Chapter 3

Jesus Christ

Fortunately, it is not up to us to provide our own solution for our sins (even though some of us think we have the solution). God the Father has a provision for sin. He has the definitive option and an adequate payment plan. There is only one way. The plan involves His Son.

Isaiah 9:6 ...a son will be given to us...

The purpose of the Son is clarified in **John 3:16.**

John 3:16 For God so loved the world, that He gave His only begotten Son, that whoever believes in Him shall not perish, but have eternal life.

This fact in history has binding results today and into the future. The grammar of the verse (**Isaiah 9:6**) in Hebrew indicates that the Son is given to us, a gift.

Yes, we are guilty. But God the Father offers us a free gift. Somebody has taken our fine and paid it for us. He has paid our debt without charging us.

Romans 6:23 For the wages of sin is death, but the free gift of God is eternal life in Christ Jesus our Lord.

And this is where the mercy, grace, and forgiveness of Jesus enters the scene. Christ loves us <u>ALL</u> in spite of our actions whatever they may be. He paid the penalty for sin. For those who believe, He has paid the fine for sin. Jesus Christ is our answer and defense.

Jesus is without sin and led a sinless life. He is a qualified defense attorney. He is able to pay the fine for sin. Based on His sinless life, He is able to die and shed sinless blood.

2 Corinthians 5:21 He made Him who knew no sin to be sin on our behalf, so that we might become the righteousness of God in Him.

1 John 3:5 You know that He appeared in order to take away sins; and in Him there is no sin.

1 Peter 2:22 He committed no sin, neither was deceit found in his mouth. Peter is quoting Isaiah 53.

It is the shedding of Christ's blood that is the forgiveness of sins. The Old Testament sacrificial system does not apply. Animal sacrifices do not ultimately pay for sin. Animal sacrifices were object lessons pointing toward the ultimate sacrifice, Jesus Christ.

Hebrews 9:12 He (Jesus) entered once for all into the holy places, not by means of the blood of goats and calves but by means of his own blood, thus securing an eternal redemption.

An Old Testament example that foreshadowed the coming of Jesus is the mercy seat on the Ark of the Covenant. His character was prophesied in the famous Temple artifact. The mercy seat is the cover or lid for the Ark of the Covenant.

Exodus 25:17 You shall make a <u>mercy seat</u> of pure gold, two and a half cubits long and one and a half cubits wide.

The Hebrew word for "mercy seat" is **kapporeth**. Per Strong's Concordance it means: mercy seat, place of atonement; the golden plate of propitiation on which the High Priest sprinkled the seat seven times on the Day of Atonement symbolically reconciling Jehovah and His chosen people; on the lid were two golden cherubim facing each other whose outstretched wings came together.

The Hebrew word **kapporeth** comes from **kopher** (means propitiatory or substitution).

The mercy seat or the lid of the Ark is a substitution for the covering of sin.

For God, the shedding of innocent blood on the mercy seat is a satisfactory substitution for sin. Only the High Priest can make the sacrifice in the presence of God.

Jesus is our High Priest who sacrificed His blood for sin.

Hebrews 4:14 Therefore, since we have a great high priest who has passed through the heavens, Jesus the Son of God, let us hold fast our confession.

Jesus Christ is the mercy seat. This gift is received only by faith. Nothing you can do. Your works don't count. You can't buy your way.

The ultimate example of God's release or remission is in His Son. Jesus forgives us of our debt, sin.

John 1:29 The next day he saw Jesus coming to him and said, "Behold, the Lamb of God who takes away the sin of the world!

Romans 5:9 Much more then, having now been justified by His blood, we shall be saved from the wrath *of God* through Him.

Believers in Christ are cleansed of sin by the innocent blood of the Lamb.

1 Peter 2:24 and He Himself bore our sins in His body on the cross, so that we might die to sin and live to righteousness; for by His wounds you were healed. Peter is quoting **Isaiah 53.**

Isaiah 53:5 But He was pierced through for our transgressions, He was crushed for our iniquities; the chastening for our well-being *fell* upon Him, and by His scourging we are healed.

Jesus Christ's work on the cross is our purification for sin. Jesus is the sacrificial paschal lamb. Christ's crown of thorns is the brushed blood on the lintel of the door. He is the shed blood on the doorposts with His outstretched arms on the cross.

John 1:29 Behold, the Lamb of God who takes away the sin of the world!

God saves us from sin via the shed blood of His Son. The fine has been paid. There are no strings or conditions attached. Our transgressions are forgiven as a matter of grace and mercy. Eternal life is a merciful, gracious gift, plain and simple.

Ephesians 1:7 In Him we have redemption through His blood, the forgiveness of our trespasses, according to the riches of His grace.

Christ's blood is the fulfillment of the propitiation or substitution. It is better than bleach. His shed blood satisfies the just nature of God. This is the only appeasement. There has to be a payment for all sin. Only the blood of Christ can wash away humanity's dross and impurities. Christ's shed blood is more powerful and cleanses better than fire. He is the one who purifies and refines. He removes the scum and the dregs.

1 John 1:7b ...and the blood of Jesus His Son cleanses us from all sin.

Romans 3:25 whom God put forward as a propitiation by his blood, to be received by faith. This was to show God's righteousness, because in his divine forbearance he had passed over former sins.

1 John 2:2 and He Himself is the propitiation for our sins; and not for ours only, but also for *those of* the whole world.

Jesus forgives all sins. There is not a list of special exemptions or conditions.

1 John 1:7 But if we walk in the light, as he is in the light, we have fellowship with one another, and the blood of Jesus his Son cleanses us from <u>all</u> sin.

The Greek word for "all" used by John is **πασ/pas**. Per Strong's Concordance it means: each, every, any, all, the whole, everyone, all things, everything. ALL sin is forgiven.

With Jesus, forgiveness of sin is not a one-time special offer. "For this year only..." No, you can come to Jesus any time you want. Now would be a good time. It does not have to be a special year or date. When Jesus dealt with sin, it was taken care of once and for all time. All people are covered if they are accepting of His effort and payment.

1 Peter 3:18 For Christ also died for sins <u>once</u> for all, *the* just for *the* unjust, so that He might bring us to God, having been put to death in the flesh, but made alive in the spirit.

Romans 6:10a For the death that He died, He died to sin <u>once</u> for all...

Hebrews 9:28 so Christ, having been offered <u>once</u> to bear the sins of many, will appear a second time, not to deal with sin but to save those who are eagerly waiting for him.

Hebrews 10:10 And by that will, we have been sanctified through the sacrifice of the body of Jesus Christ <u>once for all</u>.

The Greek word for "once" is **ηαπαξ/hapax**. It means: once, one time, once for all. Christ's one and only death is enough to cover the sins of the planet across the ages.

Chapter 3 Study Questions

Why is Jesus able to pay for the sins of humanity?

How did Jesus pay for sin?

How is Jesus like the mercy seat on the Ark of the Covenant?

What role is Jesus Christ fulfilling currently at the right hand of the Father in Heaven?

What is the significance of the shed blood of Jesus?

Are there any sins of humanity exempt from the blood of Christ?

Chapter 4

Resurrection

So, what if Jesus was not raised from the dead? What's the big deal about the resurrection? Who cares? Scripture states twice in the below verses, we are wasting our time with Christianity and the Bible if the resurrection is not true. Without the resurrection, we physically die and our bodies are eternally buried. Death wins. We are dirt and worm food. Our bodies become the byproduct of worm digestion…

Job 21:26 Together they lie down in the dust, and worms cover them.

Without Jesus' resurrection, our faith is described as "**vain**" and "**worthless**".

1 Corinthians 15:14b …your faith is also in vain.

1 Corinthians 15:17 and if Christ has not been raised, your faith is worthless; you are still in your sins.

The Greek word for "vain" is **κενοσ /kenos**. It means: empty, devoid of truth; contains nothing; empty handed; without a gift; fruitless; no purpose.

The Greek word for "worthless" is **ματαιοσ /mataios**. It means: devoid of force, truth, success, result; useless, of no purpose. - Definitions per Strong's Concordance

This is our faith without the resurrection of Christ. Without Jesus' resurrection, there is no hope for our bodies. We are dead and buried, a corrupt and purposeless mess, an empty shell.

If we are not resurrected in the future, then Christ's resurrection in the past did not occur. We have historical proof of Jesus overcoming death with hundreds of witnesses. We know what happened to Jesus. This observation is stated at least twice by Paul. That's the security and truth of our future resurrection.

1 Corinthians 15:13 But if there is no resurrection of the dead, not even Christ has been raised...

1 Corinthians 15:16 For if the dead are not raised, not even Christ has been raised;

With the resurrection of Christ, **Psalm 16:10** was prophetically fulfilled.

Psalm 16:10 For You will not abandon my soul to Sheol; nor will You allow Your Holy One to undergo decay.

With His death, Jesus did not stay in Sheol or Hades or the grave (see **Ephesians 8-10**). There was no decomposition of His body.

Acts 2:31 Foreseeing this, David spoke about the resurrection of the Christ, that He was not abandoned to Hades, nor did His body see decay.

There are two words used for the concept of "resurrection". Here is how the words can be translated from the original Greek. The first example is in the verse below.

1 Corinthians 15:13 But if there is no <u>resurrection</u> of the dead, not even Christ has been raised;

The Greek word for "resurrection" is **αναστασισ** /anastasis. It means: raising up, rising (e.g. from a seat); a rising from the dead; that of Christ; that of all men at the end of this present age. -Strong's Concordance

The second example is "raised".

1 Corinthians 15:4 and that He was buried, and that He was <u>raised</u> on the third day according to the Scriptures...

The Greek word for "raised" is **εγειρο/egeiro"**. It means: to awake, to arouse from the sleep of death, to recall the dead to life. -Strong's Concordance

The resurrection of Jesus is the power of God. The resurrection validates and authenticates Christ's death on the cross which is the payment for sin. The resurrection is dominance over death. It proved Jesus was deity. Jesus was literally raised out of, from among the dead. He is the first of the resurrection. Without the Jesus' resurrection, there is no hope for our bodies. He is the guarantee our resurrection. Without it, our faith is pointless. The promise of the resurrection is the reconnection of our body, soul, and spirit into a glorified body.

God the Father will judge the world through His Son Jesus. Based on what, the fact of the resurrection.

Acts 17:31 because He has fixed a day in which He will judge the world in righteousness through a Man whom He has appointed, having furnished proof to all men by raising Him from the dead."

Currently, Jesus is our High Priest in Heaven. He is our representative before the Father. At this time, we do not need an earthly priest. The Pope, a priest, or any other human agent on earth does not represent us before God the Father. The individual believer has direct access to God the Father via God the Son because we are sealed with God the Spirit.

Hebrews 7:24-26 but Jesus, on the other hand, because He continues forever, holds His priesthood permanently. Therefore He is able also to save forever those who draw near to God through Him, since He always lives to make intercession for them. For it was fitting for us to have such a high priest, holy, innocent, undefiled, separated from sinners and exalted above the heavens.

The gospel is not a New Testament phenomenon as some critics would have us believe. How many times have we heard, "The God of the Old Testament is a mean, cruel killer!" God is not an oppressive ogre who wants to crush you with His thumb. He has always been merciful, gracious, and forgiving. Honestly, if God smashed us like a bug any time we screwed up...would there be any humanity left? The good news has always been there. His redemption for humanity was promised from the beginning of time in the Garden of Eden. God delivered the "good news" to Satan.

Genesis 3:15 And I will put enmity between you and the woman, and between your seed and her seed; He shall bruise you on the head, and you shall bruise him on the heel.

Just in case anyone is wondering, the message of a sacrificial death for sin rings loud and clear in the Old Testament. The best example of the gospel in the Old Testament comes from the Prophet **Isaiah** about 700 years before Jesus Christ walked the earth. Look at the detail of these verses. It reads as a narrative of the events along with the accounts in **Matthew, Mark, Luke,** and **John**.

Isaiah 53:3-12 He was despised and forsaken of men, a man of sorrows and acquainted with grief; and like one from whom men hide their face He was despised, and we did not esteem Him. Surely our griefs He Himself bore, and our sorrows He carried; yet we ourselves esteemed Him stricken, smitten of God, and afflicted. But He was pierced through for our transgressions, He was crushed for our iniquities; the chastening for our well-being *fell* upon Him, and by His scourging we are healed. All of us like sheep have gone astray, each of us has turned to his own way; but the LORD has caused the iniquity of us all to fall on Him. He was oppressed and He was afflicted, yet He did not open His mouth; like a lamb that is led to slaughter, and like a sheep that is silent before its shearers, so He did not open His mouth. By oppression and judgment He was taken away; and as for His generation, who considered that He was cut off out of the land of the living for the transgression of my people, to whom the stroke *was due?* His grave was assigned

with wicked men, yet He was with a rich man in His death, because He had done no violence, nor was there any deceit in His mouth. But the LORD was pleased to crush Him, putting *Him* to grief; if He would render Himself *as* a guilt offering, He will see *His* offspring, He will prolong *His* days, and the good pleasure of the LORD will prosper in His hand. As a result of the anguish of His soul, He will see *it and* be satisfied; by His knowledge the Righteous One, My Servant, will justify the many, as He will bear their iniquities. Therefore, I will allot Him a portion with the great, and He will divide the booty with the strong; because He poured out Himself to death, and was numbered with the transgressors; yet He Himself bore the sin of many, and interceded for the transgressors.

This book the Bible, says His Son, Jesus Christ, is physically coming back in the clouds to get His people the church, at the resurrection and the rapture. Then, He will return later to establish His kingdom on earth.

And that is good news. Jesus is the Messiah, just believe it.

John 20:31 But these are written so that you may *believe* **Jesus is the Messiah, the Son of God, and by** *believing* **you may have life in His name.**

Hebrews 11:6 And without *faith* **it is impossible to please Him, for he who comes to God** *must believe* **that He is and** *that* **He is a rewarder of those who seek Him.**

Chapter 4 Study Questions

Without the resurrection, what happens to us?

The Apostle Paul describes our faith as what without the resurrection of Jesus?

In 1 Corinthians 15, what proof does the Apostle Paul offer of Christ's resurrection?

God the Father will judge the world through His Son Jesus, based on what?

Where is the first mention of the redemptive good news for humanity in the Bible?

What is the significance of the resurrection?

Chapter 5

Spring Feasts

There are seven God appointed holidays communicated through the Old Testament Law. The focus of this book is on the first three appointments. The first three spring holidays were fulfilled on the appointed holiday by Jesus Himself. The names of the feasts are known in Christendom as Passover, Unleavened Bread, and First Fruits.

Passover

The first of God's holidays is Passover or Pesach in the Hebrew. The holiday begins on the 14th day of the Hebrew month Nisan (March or April on a Gregorian calendar). There is a play on words in the original Hebrew. A **"pesach"** is an unblemished lamb which was required for the sacrifice. After the **"pesach"** was sacrificed, the blood was to be smeared on the wooden posts of the house. When God saw the blood on the door posts, He passed over or **"pasach"** and the house was spared judgment.

The original directions for the Passover were given to Moses and Aaron in Egypt. The statute and happenings are noted in **Exodus 12**. God defines the purpose of the holiday to Israel.

Exodus 12:26-27a "And when your children say to you, 'What does this rite mean to you?' you shall say, 'It is a Passover sacrifice to the LORD who passed over the houses of the sons of Israel in Egypt when He smote the Egyptians, but spared our homes.'"

Save a Place for Elijah

Malachi 4:5-6 Behold, I will send you Elijah the prophet before the great and awesome day of the LORD comes. He will restore the hearts of the fathers to their children and the hearts of the children to their fathers, so that I will not come and smite the land with a curse.

These are the last words and thoughts of the Old Testament. There would be silence for approximately 425 years...

A tradition at a Passover Seder is to leave an empty seat for the prophet Elijah. The empty seat is at the head of the table. A cup of wine is poured for Elijah should he show at the Seder. Elijah is the honored guest who is to announce the arrival of the Messiah.

Tradition has children opening the front door of the home in the hope of the arrival of Elijah. As the door is opened, the guests say... **"Blessed is he who comes in the name of the Lord."**

<u>Christ in the Passover</u>, Ceil and Moishe Rosen, Moody Press, Chicago.

John the Baptist was a type or forerunner for the first coming of Jesus Christ. Jesus Himself made the declaration.

Mark 9:12-13 And He said to them, "Elijah does first come and restore all things. And yet how is it written of the Son of Man that He will suffer many things and be treated with contempt? But I say to you that Elijah has indeed come, and they did to him whatever they wished, just as it is written of him." –Jesus.

And Jesus confirms that John the Baptist functions as if Elijah.

Matthew 11:14 "And if you are willing to accept it, John himself is Elijah who was to come." –Jesus.

...and they did to him whatever they wished...and that they did. John the Baptist was beheaded. King Herod used the excuse of a "good dance" to complete what he wanted to do anyway.

Matthew 14:10-11 He sent and had John beheaded in the prison. And his head was brought on a platter and given to the girl, and she brought it to her mother.

Jesus is coming a second time and will return to Earth. At that time, Christ will have a forerunner as He did the first time. I take it this next time it will be Elijah himself. Although he is not specifically named, Elijah is likely one of the two witnesses in **Revelation 11**. The skill set and characteristics of the witnesses are consistent with the prophet Elijah on his first mission.

See **1 Kings 17-21** and **2 Kings 1-2** for Elijah's initial career and efforts.

Revelation 11:3 And I will grant authority to my two witnesses, and they will prophesy for twelve hundred and sixty days, clothed in sackcloth.

And like John the Baptist...

Revelation 11:7 When they have finished their testimony, the beast that comes up out of the abyss will make war with them, and overcome them and kill them.

So when Elijah shows up and drinks the cup of wine at the Passover Seder, Yeshua HaMashiach is close...

Passover and Hyssop

Exodus 12:22 You shall take a bunch of <u>hyssop</u> and dip it in the blood which is in the basin, and apply some of the blood that is in the basin to the lintel and the two doorposts; and none of you shall go outside the door of his house until morning.

Hyssop is used in the directions of the Passover celebration for the Israelites.

The Hebrew word for hyssop is **'ezowb**. Per Strong's Concordance it is a plant used for medicinal and religious purposes.

Many conjectures have been formed as to what this plant really was. Some contend that it was a species of marjoram (origanum), six species of which are found in Palestine. Others with more probability think that it was the caper plant, the Capparis spinosa of Linnaeus. This plant grew in Egypt, in the desert of Sinai, and in Palestine. It was capable of producing a stem three or four feet in length. -NET Bible

Psalms 51:7 Purify me with hyssop, and I shall be clean; wash me, and I shall be whiter than snow.

Hyssop is like bleach for sin. Purify or **chata'** in the Hebrew means: to bear loss; to make a sin-offering; to purify from sin; to purify from uncleanness.

Numbers 19:18 A clean person shall take hyssop and dip *it* **in the water, and sprinkle** *it* **on the tent and on all the furnishings and on the persons who were there, and on the one who touched the bone or the one slain or the one dying** *naturally* **or the grave.**

Hyssop is required for ceremonial cleanliness when a person came in contact with dead bodies or dead animals. Cleanliness kept the Israelite from being cut off from the assembly.

Leviticus 14:52 He shall thus cleanse the house with the blood of the bird and with the running water, along with the live bird and with the cedar wood and with the hyssop and with the scarlet string.

Another example of ritual cleaning involves the use of hyssop in a leprous house. Hyssop is involved in the law of leprosy (**Leviticus 14:33-57**).

Jesus Christ's work on the cross is our purification for sin. **John 1:29 Behold, the Lamb of God who takes away the sin of the world!** Jesus is the sacrificial paschal lamb. Christ's crown of thorns is the brushed blood on the lintel of the door. He is the shed blood on the doorposts with His outstretched arms on the cross.

John 19:29 A jar full of sour wine was standing there; so they put a sponge full of the sour wine upon *a <u>branch of hyssop</u>* and brought it up to His mouth.

1 John 1:7b ... and the blood of Jesus His Son cleanses us from all sin.

Unleavened Bread

The second of God's holidays is Unleavened Bread or Chag haMatazt in the Hebrew. The holiday begins on the 15th of Nisan and runs for seven days.

The directions of Unleavened Bread are noted in **Exodus 12:15-20**. The focus of the week is to live a life without leaven, the symbol for sin. Leaven is not to be in the house. Leaven products are not to be consumed. Bread without yeast, **matzah**, is to be eaten.

Exodus 12:15-20 Seven days you shall eat unleavened bread. On the first day you shall remove leaven out of your houses, for if anyone eats what is leavened, from the first day until the seventh day, that person shall be cut off from Israel. On the first day you shall hold a holy assembly, and on the seventh day a holy assembly. No work shall be done on those days. But what everyone needs to eat, that alone may be prepared by you. And you shall observe the Feast of Unleavened Bread, for on this very day I brought your hosts out of the land of Egypt. Therefore you shall observe this day, throughout your generations, as a statute forever. In the first *month*, on the fourteenth day of the month at evening, you shall eat unleavened bread, until the twenty-first day of the month at evening. Seven days there shall be no leaven found in your houses; for whoever eats what is leavened, that person shall be cut off from the congregation of Israel, whether *he is* an alien or a native of the land. You shall not eat anything leavened; in all your dwellings you shall eat unleavened bread.

What does the **matzah** look like? In the most fundamental Judaism homes, **matzah** is an irregular, round shaped piece of bread. It resembles a cracker or wafer in thickness. There are even rows of tiny holes on the wafer bread. The cracker-like bread appears to be striped.

Isaiah 53:5 But He was pierced through for our transgressions, He was crushed for our iniquities; the chastening for our well-being *fell* upon Him, and by His scourging we are healed.

1 Peter 2:24 and He Himself bore our sins in His body on the cross, so that we might die to sin and live to righteousness; for by His wounds you were healed. Peter is quoting Isaiah 53.

Jesus is the unleavened bread. He is the bread of life.

John 6:35 Jesus said to them, "I am the bread of life; he who comes to Me will not hunger, and he who believes in Me will never thirst.

John 6:48 I am the bread of life.

John 6:50-51 This is the bread which comes down out of heaven, so that one may eat of it and not die. I am the living bread that came down out of heaven; if anyone eats of this bread, he will live forever; and the bread also which I will give for the life of the world is My flesh.

Unleavened Bread: Broken & Hidden Matzah

Exodus 12:19 Seven days there shall be no leaven found in your houses; for whoever eats what is leavened, that person shall be cut off from the congregation of Israel, whether he is an alien or a native of the land.

This is the original Spring cleaning. Get the sin out of your life. The holiday is for seven days. The focus of the week is to live a life without leaven, the symbol for sin. Leaven is not to be in the house. Leaven products are not to be consumed. Goodbye to a loaf of bread, biscuits, and donuts.

Matzah has taken its place as the unleavened bread. At a Passover Seder, the matzah is broken before the meal. Part of the matzah is taken and wrapped in a cloth napkin. The cloth with the unleavened bread is taken away and hidden. At the end of the Seder, the unleavened bread is returned and eaten to close out the ceremony.

1 John 3:5 You know that He appeared in order to take away sins; and in Him there is no sin.

Does this sound familiar? Jesus, the sinless man, was broken in death. His body was without sin. Christ is the unleavened bread.

1 Corinthians 11:24 and when He had given thanks, He broke it and said, "This is My body, which is for you; do this in remembrance of Me."

After He died, the body of Jesus was wrapped in a linen cloth. He was hidden or buried as the unleavened bread.

Mark 15:46 Joseph bought a linen cloth, took Him down, wrapped Him in the linen cloth and laid Him in a tomb which had been hewn out in the rock; and he rolled a stone against the entrance of the tomb.

Christ was raised from the dead and resurrected. The unleavened bread is returned. Those who partake in Him shall have everlasting life.

Mark 16:6 And he said to them, "Do not be amazed; you are looking for Jesus the Nazarene, who has been crucified. He has risen; He is not here; behold, here is the place where they laid Him."

Jesus Christ is the body without sin. He is the truth.

1 Corinthians 5:7-8 Clean out the old leaven so that you may be a new lump, just as you are in fact unleavened. For Christ our Passover also has been sacrificed. Therefore let us celebrate the feast, not with old leaven, nor with the leaven of malice and wickedness, but with the unleavened bread of sincerity and truth.

First Fruits

The third of God's holidays is First Fruits or Reshit Katzir in the Hebrew. The one day holiday begins on the day after the Sabbath or Sunday on our calendar.

The directions for First Fruits are noted in **Leviticus 23:9-14.**

Leviticus 23:9-14 Then the LORD spoke to Moses, saying, "Speak to the sons of Israel and say to them, 'When you enter the land which I am going to give to you and reap its harvest, then you shall bring in the sheaf of the first fruits of your harvest to the priest. He shall wave the sheaf before the LORD for you to be accepted; on the day after the sabbath the priest shall wave it. Now on the day when you wave the sheaf, you shall offer a male lamb one year old without defect for a burnt offering to the LORD. Its grain offering shall then be two-tenths *of an ephah* **of fine flour mixed with oil, an offering by fire to the LORD** *for* **a soothing aroma, with its drink offering, a fourth of a hin of wine. Until this same day, until you have brought in the offering of your God, you shall eat neither bread nor roasted grain nor new growth. It is to be a perpetual statute throughout your generations in all your dwelling places.**

The priest is to make a barley offering of the first portion of the harvest to the Lord. The priest intervenes of behalf of the people. The reality of the holiday for the people of Israel is this. The people bring their grain sheaf to the priest. They are to sacrifice a lamb without blemish. The offering is also to be presented with bread and wine.

1 Corinthians 15:20-24a But now Christ has been raised from the dead, the <u>first fruits</u> of those who are asleep. For since by a man *came* **death, by a man also** *came* **the resurrection of the dead. For as in Adam all die, so also in Christ all will be made alive. But each in his own order: Christ the first fruits, after that those who are Christ's at His coming...**

So people ask, what are the "first fruits"? This is a reference to the Lord's Festival. It is as known as different titles. It is called the "Feast of First Fruits" in Christianity. In Hebraic Judaism, it is known as "Reshit Katzir". In a Jewish mindset it means, the beginning of the harvest. The harvest is resurrected bodies. First Fruits is the third of the LORD's spring holidays.

First Fruits has its roots in the Old Testament after the Jews Exodus out of Egypt. The Jewish people were given this appointment from God after leaving Egypt.

There are specific directions as to the administration of this holiday. Traditionally, the first fruit to be harvested is barley. The grain is to be presented before God as a fine flour mixed with oil and baked. Translation, a barley bread was baked without yeast. Yeast is symbolically sin. The drink offering is wine. Contained in these instructions is a foreshadowing of the elements of communion, bread and wine. Who proclaimed to be the "bread of life"?

Another condition, a perfect lamb was presented and sacrificed. Jesus is called the Lamb of God at least 27 times in the **Book of Revelation** alone. We know He was sacrificed on a cross. Christ, the seed of grain, was planted in a tomb and resurrected a glorified, incorruptible body.

This is to take place one day after the Sabbath, the first day of the week, or Sunday. God tells the Jewish people this festival is to be completed continually where ever you live. Give thanks to God before eating.

Jesus is the initial harvest of the resurrection. There was a wave of believers in Jesus who were resurrected in Jerusalem after Christ.

Matthew 27:52-53 The tombs also were opened. And many bodies of the saints who had fallen asleep were raised, and coming out of the tombs after his resurrection they went into the holy city and appeared to many.

Christ, as high priest, presented and waived this resurrected harvest before the Father in Heaven.

These spring holidays tell the story of Jesus at His first coming. He was the Passover Lamb that was sacrificed. He was buried before the Sabbath began. The Feast of Unleavened Bread was celebrated on the Sabbath. And He was resurrected on the first day of the week in accordance with the Feast of First Fruits. The Jewish people participated in this holiday for thousands of years from the time of Moses. These spring feasts were literally fulfilled to the day in the person of Jesus.

Chapter 5 Study Guide

Name the first 3 God appointed Spring Feasts.

Who is the forerunner to the Messiah for His first and second coming?

Symbolically, what is the role of hyssop?

What is matzah and how is it like Jesus Christ? List as many examples as possible.

Leaven is a symbol for what?

Name the elements associated with the feast of First Fruits.

Who do the elements of First Fruits point towards?

Chapter 6

Fullness of Time

Galatians 4:4-5 But when <u>the fullness of time</u> had come, God sent forth his Son, born of woman, born under the law, to redeem those who were under the law, so that we might receive adoption as sons.

...the fullness of time... God had specific times in mind for the literal events that make up the gospel message from before the beginning of the creation. He made the Heavens, the sun, the moon, and the Earth and their fixed orbits for those times. Absolute deadlines were ordained and had to specifically occur as He created.

God gave His word and plan to Moses roughly 1,600 years before the birth of Jesus. The Jewish people completed yearly ceremonies to mark the celebration of God's appointed holidays according to their time.

Think of all the factors and the coordination of events. Think of all the people involved and their actions, Jesus Himself, the Sanhedrin, the High Priest, Pilate and his wife, Roman soldiers, Peter, John, the other apostles, Judas, Joseph of Arimathea, the Jewish people, Mary, Mary Magdalene and the list goes on and on and on. Despite all these individual wills, God is in control of history and time. And it all happened perfectly in **the fullness of time**.

Philippians 2:5-8 Have this mind among yourselves, which is yours in Christ Jesus, who, though He was in the form of God, did not count equality with God a thing to be grasped, but emptied Himself, by taking the form of a servant, being born in the likeness of men. And being found in human form, He humbled Himself by becoming obedient to the point of death, even death on a cross.

Christ is deity and humanity all rolled into one. Jesus was born under and subjected to the Law. He lived and abided under the same rules as everyone else. His deity did not exclude Him. As you read the next section of this book, look and see how Jesus related to the Law during the last week of His life. The main focus includes God's spring appointed feasts.

Jesus was crucified at a specific time. He was obedient to the point of death. Christ had to be dead and buried before the sun set or He would have been cursed. He was buried at a specific time. And He was raised at a specific time. Christ fulfilled the Spring Feasts of the Law on time. If He did not keep and fulfill even one little detail, the whole thing falls apart. And we worship in vein.

Apart from Jesus, we as humanity are all under God's Law whether we believe it or like it or agree with it. Humanity has a serious legal problem with eternal consequences.

So what is the point of all of this? He loves us. He bought us, **so that we might receive adoption as sons.**

And this is how it happened, in **the fullness of time...**

Creation of Time

Genesis 1:14 Then God said, "Let there be lights in the expanse of the heavens to separate the day from the night, and let them be for signs and for seasons and for days and years...

God has a plan and a purpose for His creation from the beginning. These are not random events that occurred by chance from an explosion of a singularity. The cosmos was not blown willy nilly into existence.

Here we go again, another day and another difference in how God created and man postulates over the creation. The Big Bang says an explosion took place approximately 15 billion years ago. Biblical genealogies back to Adam calculate the earth is less than 10,000 years old.

Science says the sun was present before the earth. God spoke the earth into existence on the first day and the sun was created on the fourth day.

Science says that the sun was present before other light on the earth. God says there was light which was created on day one other than the sun. This light separated day from night.

Science says the stars were before the earth. God says the stars were created on day four after the creation of the earth on day one.

Science says that the earth was created at the same time as the other planets. God says the earth was created first and the other planets were created later on day four.

Observations and distinctions are from www.answersingenesis.org .

God does draw a distinction from the "light" created on day one and "lights" created on day four. The following is an excerpt from Dr. Henry Morris' Defender Bible, www.icr.org

On the first day, God had said: "Let there be light" (Hebrew *or*). Now He says: "Let there be lights" (*ma-or*). Light energy was activated first, but now great masses of material (part of the "earth" elements created on the first day) were gathered together in one of the firmaments, or spaces, of the cosmos–the space beyond the waters above the space adjacent to the earth. These great bodies were set burning in complex chemical and nuclear reactions, to serve henceforth as "light-givers" for the earth.

Dr. Morris, www.icr.org , also has this observation regarding the "seasons".

The establishment of "seasons" (and these were not simply religious seasons, but actual climatological seasons) indicates that the earth was formed with an axial inclination from the beginning, for this is the basic cause of its seasons.

God is very clear about the intent and purpose of the creation of these heavenly bodies.

Isaiah 40:26 Lift up your eyes on high and see who has created these *stars*, the One who leads forth their host by number, He calls them all by name; because of the greatness of His might and the strength of *His* power, not one *of them* is missing.

As of 2010, Universe Today and European Space Agency have attempted to estimate the number of stars in the universe. The Milky Way Galaxy has approximately 200 billion stars. The average galaxy contains between 10^{11} and 10^{12} stars. Astronomers estimate there are approximately 100 billion to 1 trillion (10% variance at best) galaxies in the universe. When the number of galaxies is multiplied by the number of stars per galaxy, you get between 10^{22} and 10^{24} stars in the universe. Remember, this is the best estimate of man based on what he can observe. There are likely more.

Consider **Isaiah 40:26** from a semantic perspective. Various linguistic estimates account for one million words in the English language. Think of the vocabulary of God to name **ALL** of these stars. All stars are accounted and personally named. Our vocabulary is ridiculously limited in comparison. This number of stars created and noted makes **Matthew 10:30** a walk in the park from a counting perspective.

Matthew 10:30 But the very hairs of your head are all numbered. –Jesus

How big is the universe? What is the scale of the universe? Is it round or flat or some other shape? Is the universe finite or infinite? The reality of the situation is we don't know for sure. What we think we know is what we can observe. Tom Murphy (January of 2006) does provide some points of comparison in a paper he has written. Consider these points.

1) The moon is 1.25 light seconds from earth.
2) The sun is about 8 light minutes from earth.

3) Jupiter is about 40 light minutes from sun.
4) Pluto is about 5.5 light hours from the sun.
5) The center of the Milky Way is about 25,000 light years away.
6) The galaxy Andromeda is about 2,000,000 light years away.
7) The edge of the visible universe is about 13,700,000,000 light years away.

http://physics.ucsd.edu/~tmurphy/phys10/universe.pdf

This is the universe God has created.

Jeremiah 23:24 "Can a man hide himself in hiding places so I do not see him?" declares the LORD. "Do I not fill the heavens and the earth?" declares the LORD.

If we were capable of going to Andromeda, God is there. If we were to hide anywhere in the Milky Way, God is there. God is ridiculously immense and He is everywhere. He is omnipresent. There is no place in the universe or on Earth where God is not. It is impossible to hide from God. Regardless of the darkness of space, God is there and He can find us.

There are prophetic implications of **Genesis 1:14**. There will come a time in the future where God's purpose in the heavens will be on display to humanity during the Tribulation.

There are multiple purposes for these lights and they are stated clearly. One, the lights are to separate day and night. Two, they are signs. Three, they are time markers (seasons, holidays, appointments, days, and years).

...let them be for signs and for seasons...

The Hebrew word for "seasons" is **mow`ed** (singular); **mow`edim** (plural). It means: appointed place, appointed time, meeting; appointed time; sacred season, set feast, appointed season; appointed meeting; appointed sign or signal; tent of meeting (definition provided by Strong's Concordance).

These purposes are repeated and we are reminded throughout the Bible. The information is not contained specifically to **Genesis**. Look at a star filled sky at night. Granted, man has blinded himself from God's truth with all the city lights. The night sky speaks to the honor, splendor, greatness, and abundance of God. The heavens are God's handiwork. The heavens display His discernment, perception, and skill. It tells of the order and power of God. It gives us insight to who He is.

Psalms 19:1-2 The heavens are telling of the glory of God; and their expanse is declaring the work of His hands. Day to day pours forth speech, and night to night reveals knowledge.

The four seasons were ordained from the point of creation.

Psalms 104:19 He made the moon for the seasons; the sun knows the place of its setting.

Psalms 74:16-17 Yours is the day, Yours also is the night; You have prepared the light and the sun. You have established all the boundaries of the earth; You have made summer and winter.

The Jewish calendar is based on three astronomical phenomena. These three are independent of each other.

1) **Rotation of the Earth about its axis (a day):**
2) **Revolution of the moon about the Earth (a month):** The average time for the moon to revolve around the Earth is 29.5 days. A pure lunar calendar has a minimum of 354 days in a year.
3) **Revolution of the Earth about the sun (a year):** The Earth revolves around the sun in about 365 1/4 days. A pure solar calendar has 12.4 lunar months.

The Jewish calendar coordinates all three of these astronomical phenomena. It is based on moon cycles instead of sun cycles. "Leap months" are added to sync up with sun cycles. Prior to the 4th century, the calendar was determined by observation. The calendar has been calculated mathematically since 4th century. Years are numbered from creation.

A Hebrew Year always contains 12 Hebrew months in a regular year or 13 Hebrew months in a leap year.

http://www.jewfaq.org/calendar.htm
http://www.hebrew4christians.com/Holidays/Calendar/calendar.html

The context of **Exodus 12:2** is God giving Moses and Aaron directions prior to the first Passover and eventual exodus from Egypt. This is how and when God determined His New Year.

Exodus 12:2 This month shall be the beginning of months for you; it is to be the first month of the year to you.

The Biblical or Religious New Year begins at the moment of sunset at Jerusalem, on the evening of the first potentially visible crescent moon (Rosh Chodesh) beginning Day 1 of Month 1. The spring equinox is the demarcation point governing the solar cycle. A Biblical New Year can begin before or after the spring equinox.

The month of Nisan is the beginning of the religious or spiritual year in a Hebrew calendar. The beginning of the civil year is in the seventh month of Tishri. These are two calendars at work in the Hebrew.

Moses later referred to this month as Abib.

Exodus 13:4 On this day in the month of Abib, you are about to go forth.

Per Strong's Concordance, Abib means: fresh, young barley ears; month of ear-forming, of greening of crop, of growing green; month of Exodus and Passover.

The month is called Nisan in **Nehemiah 2:1 And it came about in the month Nisan...** It means "their flight". Israel took "their flight" out of Egypt in Nisan. The meaning of month Nisan is a reminder to Israel. Abib is a reminder to the time of the year, during the first fruits of the barley harvest.

As the harvest cycle goes with the Hebrews, barley is the first crop harvested in the spring or the "first fruits". And who is considered the "first fruits"?

1 Corinthians 15:20 But now Christ has been raised from the dead, the first fruits of those who are asleep.

The religious new year (Rosh Chodashim) begins at the sighting of the new moon (Rosh Chodesh). It is also located specifically on the spring equinox.

The month of Nisan is synonymous with the constellation of the lamb in the Hebrew Mazzaroth.

http://www.hebrew4christians.com/Holidays/Spring_Holidays/Rosh_Chodashim/rosh_chodashim.html

Exodus 13:10 Therefore, you shall keep this ordinance (Unleavened Bread) at its appointed time from year to year.

The first day of Unleavened Bread never occurs before the spring equinox. The rule of the equinox always places Day 15 (Feast of Unleavened Bread) of Month 1 on or after the spring equinox.

The first day of Unleavened Bread on Day 15 of Month 1 is the critical day for calculating a Hebrew Year. This ensures all three festivals take place within a single year as The LORD (Yahweh) specified.

Deuteronomy 16:16 Three times in a year all your males shall appear before the Lord your God in the place which He chooses, at the Feast of Unleavened Bread and at the Feast of Weeks and at the Feast of Booths, and they shall not appear before the Lord empty-handed.

Man cannot follow God's directions when it comes to marking time. Our western Gregorian calendar is a solar calendar. Discrepancy and confusion reigns.

This is not some cute, little story that is made up by primitive man trying to explain his surroundings and how things came to be. It is not a limited philosophical and/or intellectual understanding. It has ramifications for the history and future of planet earth. The entirety of the Bible is a master plan that started **"in the beginning"**. For all we know, these ramifications could be coming sooner than we think.

What time is it?

Sun, moon, stars, heavenlies…God's time piece.

March 20, 2015 on a Gregorian calendar, the beginning of the Hebrew religious new year on Nisan 1 was unique. Three events occurred on the same day: spring equinox, a solar eclipse, and a super moon.

http://www.independent.co.uk/news/science/solar-eclipse-supermoon-spring-equinox-friday-will-see-three-rare-celestial-events-10111592.html

"Experts" have stated this celestial alignment is very rare and happens once every 100,000 years. "Experts" are encouraged to look at math and science as related to the work of Johannes Kepler's Laws of Planetary Motion. Thanks to the German astronomer and mathematician, he developed equations to determine the exact location of the sun, moon, planets, and stars in time and space.

When these equations are utilized (by hand or computer), there is a surprise for the "experts". March 20, 2015 (Nisan 1) was not the first time a spring equinox and a solar eclipse occur on the Hebrew religious new year. This phenomenon also occurred in the spring of 33 AD on March 20 (Nisan 1).

https://sites.google.com/site/calendarstudies/bible-studies/bible_study_year_of_crucifixion

Two weeks later in 33 AD, Jesus died as the "Passover" lamb. He was buried as "unleavened bread". And He was raised from the dead as the "first fruits".

Chapter 6 Study Guide

What are your thoughts on the phrase, **the fullness of time**?

Describe the differences in God's creation account versus scientific accounts.

Compare God's vocabulary to humanity.

What physical size does God attribute to Himself?

What are the purposes of the lights in the Heavens per God?

The Jewish calendar is based on three astronomical phenomena. Name them.

According to God, when does the New Year begin?

Describe God's clock.

Chapter 7

Passion Week

Passover, Nisan 10-13, 33 AD

Exodus 12:1-6 Now the Lord said to Moses and Aaron in the land of Egypt, "This month shall be the beginning of months for you; it is to be the first month of the year to you. Speak to all the congregation of Israel, saying, 'On the tenth of this month they are each one to take a lamb for themselves, according to their fathers' households, a lamb for each household. Now if the household is too small for a lamb, then he and his neighbor nearest to his house are to take one according to the number of persons *in them*; **according to what each man should eat, you are to divide the lamb. Your lamb shall be an unblemished male a year old; you may take it from the sheep or from the goats. You shall keep it until the fourteenth day of the same month...**

These directions were given to Moses by God roughly 1,600 years before the birth of Christ. The setting was Egypt prior to the Exodus. Moving forward, the Jewish people are to complete this ordinance every year on these dates.

The focus of this post is the correlation of the dates noted in **Exodus 12** and the dates noted in the Passion Week of Christ.

On the tenth of this month they are each one to take a lamb for themselves... You shall keep it until the fourteenth day of the same month.

The directions to the Jewish people are straight forward. The first month of the religious year is Nisan. On Nisan 10, take a lamb and inspect it for four days. Make sure the lamb is unblemished. The time frame is Nisan 10, 11, 12, and 13.

Fast forward over 1,500 years, Jesus enters Jerusalem on Palm Sunday. The date is Sunday, Nisan 9, 33 AD. Jesus is the sacrificial lamb of the Passover.

We know Jesus entered Jerusalem on Palm Sunday from **John 12:1 Jesus, therefore, six days before the Passover, came to Bethany where Lazarus was, whom Jesus had raised from the dead.**

A Hebrew Calendar of 33 AD tells us Passover was on Friday, Nisan 14. Six days before Passover is Saturday or the Sabbath, Nisan 8. Scripture tells us Jesus is in Bethany on Saturday, Nisan 8. Bethany is east of Jerusalem approximately 1.5 miles. The Mount of Olives sits between Bethany and Jerusalem. He is visiting Mary, Martha, and Lazarus.

John 12:12 On the next day the large crowd who had come to the feast, when they heard that Jesus was coming to Jerusalem...

The next day is Sunday, Nisan 9. Jesus enters Jerusalem on Palm Sunday. Jesus only looked around the Temple on Nisan 9. He did not subject Himself to criticism or analysis from religious leaders by His actions on this day. Jesus did not enter Jerusalem for inspection on Palm Sunday. He left and went back to Bethany.

Mark 11:11 Jesus entered Jerusalem *and came* into the temple; and after looking around at everything, He left for Bethany with the twelve, since it was already late.

If Jesus had cleared the temple on Sunday, He would have been in the "pen" of Jerusalem for inspection five days instead of four days as indicated in **Exodus 12**. The law would not have been followed. He would have sinned.

Mark 11:12 On the next day, when they had left Bethany, He became hungry.

The next day is Monday, Nisan 10. From this point forward, Jesus was inspected for imperfections. Then He cleared the Temple. He was questioned and tested. He was examined and challenged by religious leaders, other Jews, and Greeks on Monday, Nisan 10 through Thursday, Nisan 13 for four days (March 29 – April 2, 33 AD on a Gregorian calendar). He was found to be without blemish or flaw.

http://www.torahcalendar.com/Calendar.asp?YM=Y33M1

Passover, Nisan 14, Friday, 33 AD

John 19:31 Then the Jews, because it was the day of preparation, so that the bodies would not remain on the cross on the <u>Sabbath</u> (for that <u>Sabbath</u> was a high day), asked Pilate that their legs might be broken, and *that* they might be taken away.

The Sabbath is Saturday. The day before Saturday is Friday. The Jews wanted to make sure everyone was dead before the Sabbath.

John 18:39 "But you have a custom that I release someone for you at the <u>Passover</u>; do you wish then that I release for you the King of the Jews?" – Pilate

John 19:14 Now it was the day of preparation for the <u>Passover</u>; it was about the sixth hour. And he said to the Jews, "Behold, your King!" – Pilate

Luke 22:15 And He said to them, "I have earnestly desired to eat this <u>Passover</u> with you before I suffer… -Jesus.

Remember the sun had already set. The new day had begun and it was early Friday. With God, the next day starts when the sun sets on the previous day (**Genesis 1, Creation Week**).

Luke 23:54 It was the preparation day, and the <u>Sabbath</u> was about to begin.

Mark 15:42 When evening had already come, because it was the preparation day, that is, the day before the <u>Sabbath</u>…

The context of these 2 verses (**Luke 23, Mark 15**) is the preparation of Jesus' body in the tomb before sundown. There was a mad dash to get Jesus off of the cross and buried before the Sabbath. It was not yet Saturday, so it had to be Friday.

Jesus, the Passover lamb, died the day before the Sabbath on Friday.

Passover, Nisan 14, 9 AM – 3 PM, 33 AD

Exodus 29:38-39 Now this is what you shall offer on the altar: two one-year old lambs each day, continuously. The one lamb you shall offer in the morning and the other lamb you shall offer at twilight...

There are two sacrifices per day. One is in the morning and one is in the afternoon at twilight. The daily sacrifices (morning and evening) are to be given with a bread and wine offering.

Exodus 29:40-42 And with the first lamb a tenth measure of fine flour mingled with a fourth of a hin of beaten oil, and a fourth of a hin of wine for a drink offering. The other lamb you shall offer at twilight, and shall offer with it a grain offering and its drink offering, as in the morning, for a pleasing aroma, a food offering to the LORD. It shall be a regular burnt offering throughout your generations at the entrance of the tent of meeting before the LORD, where I will meet with you, to speak to you there.

The daily offering directions are restated.

Numbers 28:1-8 The LORD spoke to Moses, saying, "Command the people of Israel and say to them, 'My offering, my food for my food offerings, my pleasing aroma, you shall be careful to offer to me at its appointed time.' And you shall say to them, This is the food offering that you shall offer to the LORD: two male lambs a year old without blemish, day by day, as a regular offering. The one lamb you shall offer in the morning, and the other lamb you shall offer at twilight; also a tenth of an ephah of fine flour for a grain offering, mixed with a quarter of a hin of beaten oil. It is a regular burnt offering, which was ordained at Mount Sinai for a pleasing aroma, a food offering to the LORD. Its drink offering shall be a quarter of a hin for each lamb. In the Holy Place you shall pour out a drink offering of strong drink to

the LORD. **The other lamb you shall offer at twilight. Like the grain offering of the morning, and like its drink offering, you shall offer it as a food offering, with a pleasing aroma to the LORD.**

This sacrifice is to be done **continuously** or **tamid** in the Hebrew. Per Strong's Concordance, **tamid** means: continuity, perpetuity, to stretch, continually, continuously (as adverb).

The book of **Acts** offers a clue as to the time of the evening sacrifice.

Acts 3:1 Now Peter and John were going up to the temple at the ninth *hour*, the hour of prayer.

To the Hebrew, the ninth hour of daylight is 3 p.m. in the afternoon. The hour of prayer was also the time of the afternoon sacrifice (Josephus, Antiquities of the Jews; Mishnah; Philo of Alexandria).

More details regarding the timing of **twilight** later.

The Hebrew word for "morning" is **boqer**. Per Strong's, it means: morning, break of day; of end of night; of coming of daylight; of coming of sunrise; of beginning of day; of bright joy after night of distress (fig.).

This is the same word on day one, in the beginning...**Genesis 1:5 God called the light day, and the darkness He called night. And there was evening and there was <u>morning</u>, one day.**

A specific time is not indicated in the Bible for the specific time of the morning sacrifice. Extra Biblical sources such as Josephus, Philo, and the Mishnah (oral teaching of the Mosaic Law) indicate the morning, daily sacrifice took place at the third hour of daylight or 9 a.m.

Moving forward roughly 1,500 years from Moses and the Law. The day is Nisan 14, 33 AD.

Mark 15:25 It was the third hour when they crucified Him.

Mark 15:34, 37 At the ninth hour Jesus cried out with a loud voice, "ELOI, ELOI, LAMA SABACHTHANI?" which is translated, "MY GOD, MY GOD, WHY HAVE YOU FORSAKEN ME?" And Jesus uttered a loud cry, and breathed His last.

The crucifixion started at the third hour of daylight or 9 a.m. He died at the ninth hour of daylight or 3 p.m. These are the same times as the perpetual sacrifice as directed by God to Moses in **Exodus 29** and **Numbers 28**.

While Christ was on the cross, the oral teachings (Mishnah) and prayers of the priests in the Temple focused on four topics: redemption, forgiveness, the coming of the Messiah, and the resurrection of the dead. The priests and people prayed these topics every day at the time of the morning and evening sacrifice.

http://www.thesacredpage.com/2010/04/jewish-roots-of-jesus-passion-and-death.html

The directions and ritual of the continual, daily sacrifice from the Mosaic Law scream, **"JESUS"**!

Jesus' death on the cross is the perpetual and eternal sacrifice for all of time. Sin happens every day. Today in the church age, we commemorate His death by communion with the elements of bread and wine. His death is the **"tamid"** sacrifice for sin.

Passover, Nisan 14, Noon – 3 PM, 33 AD

Matthew 27:45 Now from the sixth hour darkness fell upon all the land until the ninth hour.

Mark 15:33 When the sixth hour came, darkness fell over the whole land until the ninth hour.

Luke 23:44-45 It was now about the sixth hour, and darkness fell over the whole land until the ninth hour, because the sun was obscured; and the veil of the temple was torn in two.

This three-hour period of darkness is one clue that confirms the year of Christ's death.

Hebrews mark time the following way. The sun comes up in the first hour. The sun sets in the twelfth hour. Midday or noon is the sixth hour. The ninth hour is 3 o'clock in a western way of thinking. As we view time in a western sense, darkness fell upon the land at noon and remained until 3 p.m.

The event described in the Bible was not a solar eclipse. An eclipse of the sun only occurs when the moon is directly between the sun and the Earth, a new moon phase. The day of the crucifixion was the day before Passover. The spring holiday occurs during a full moon. The moon was on the far side of the Earth away from the sun. A solar eclipse can last only seven and a half minutes in any one place. Darkness in the verses of the Bible lasted three hours.

We know there was seismic activity in the region on the day of Christ's death from Scripture and extra biblical historians. This region of the world is noted with tectonic and volcanic activity.

Matthew 27:51 And behold, the veil of the temple was torn in two from top to bottom; and the earth shook and the rocks were split.

Matthew 27:54 Now the centurion, and those who were with him keeping guard over Jesus, when they saw the earthquake and the things that were happening, became very frightened and said, "Truly this was the Son of God!"

Secular historians report a failure of the sun during the middle of the day. Below is an example.

In the fourth year of the 202nd Olympiad, a failure of the sun took place greater than any previously known, and night came on at the sixth hour of the day (noon), so that stars actually appeared in the sky; and a great earthquake took place in Bithynia and overthrew the greater part of Niceaea,"— TRALLIANUS, OLYMPIADES

This event was confirmed by many other historians. Here is a brief list: Phlegon (Greek), Julius Africanus, Thallus, Eusibis, Syncellus, Jerom, Maximus, and the list goes on and on...

http://www.bethlehemstar.net/the-day-of-the-cross/peters-argument/

http://www.freechristianteaching.org/modules/smartsection/item.php?itemid=184#axzz3UUQWaXsE

Bithynia is modern day Turkey near the capital of Istanbul or historical Constantinople. Niceaea is the region of northwest Turkey.

If the sun went dark in the middle of the day in the 21st century, there would be a significant historical record of the event. It would be well documented. I can almost guarantee this. People would literally freak out if the day turned to dark and there was no solar eclipse scheduled. Put yourself in Jerusalem at the event of the cross in that day. Eerie, eerie, eerie...

The Bible confirms secular history. The sun went dark at noon. The year was 33 AD. Christ was on the cross at that time.

Passover, Nisan 14, Twilight, 33 AD

Exodus 12:5-6 Your lamb shall be an unblemished male a year old; you may take it from the sheep or from the goats. You shall keep it until the fourteenth day of the same month, then the whole assembly of the congregation of Israel is to kill it at twilight.

The point is made clearly. The Passover lamb is to be sacrificed on Nisan 14 at **twilight.**

Leviticus 23:5 In the first month, on the fourteenth day of the month at twilight is the LORD'S Passover.

Numbers 9:3 On the fourteenth day of this month, at twilight, you shall observe it at its appointed time; you shall observe it according to all its statutes and according to all its ordinances.

Numbers 9:5 They observed the Passover in the first *month,* **on the fourteenth day of the month, at twilight, in the wilderness of Sinai; according to all that the LORD had commanded Moses, so the sons of Israel did.**

Numbers 9:11 In the second month on the fourteenth day at twilight, they shall observe it; they shall eat it with unleavened bread and bitter herbs.

The Hebrew word for twilight is `ereb. Per Strong's Concordance, it means: evening, night, sunset.

This is the same word on day one, in the beginning...**Genesis 1:5 God called the light day, and the darkness He called night. And there was <u>evening</u> and there was morning, one day.**

So, the question is... "When is it officially twilight?" There is much debate about the meaning of this.

...to kill it at twilight. The phrase literally stated, **to kill between the two evenings**. The issue: when does one sacrifice the Passover lamb? Scholars have often interpreted this phrase as idiomatic language to mean a period of time before darkness.

Darkness was ending after 3:00 p.m.

Matthew 27:45 Now from the sixth hour darkness fell upon all the land until the ninth hour.

Jesus died at or briefly after 3:00 p.m.

Mark 15:34, 37 At the ninth hour Jesus cried out with a loud voice, "ELOI, ELOI, LAMA SABACHTHANI?" which is translated, "MY GOD, MY GOD, WHY HAVE YOU FORSAKEN ME?" And Jesus uttered a loud cry, and breathed His last.

Time allowed to take Him off the cross, prepare His body, and bury Him in the tomb before sun down. Sunset in Jerusalem on Nisan 14 was 6:00 p.m. local time (no day light saving time or "springing forward" back in the day). Subtract one hour from time charts to account for day light saving time. The sun sets at 6:00 p.m. on April 3 in Jerusalem.

http://www.timeanddate.com/sun/israel/jerusalem?month=4

Jesus had to be buried before sun down. The setting of the sun marked the beginning of the next day according to God (**Genesis 1, Creation Week**). He had to be buried before the beginning of the Sabbath in accordance with the Law.

The reality is Jesus literally died between the two evenings on Nisan 14, 33 AD. That afternoon had two evenings. It was dark from noon to 3 p.m.

Mark 15:33 When the sixth hour came, darkness fell over the whole land until the ninth hour.

He died at the twilight of the first period of darkness. The sun reappeared. Then the sun set at 6:00 p.m. local time.

Approximately 1,500 years after Moses was given the Law, Jesus' sacrificial death fulfilled the requirements of the Passover lamb figuratively and literally, to the hour and to the minute.

Unleavened Bread, Nisan 15, Saturday, 33 AD

The second of God's holidays is **Unleavened Bread** or **Chag haMatazt** in the Hebrew. The holiday begins on the 15th of Nisan and runs for seven days.

The directions for Unleavened Bread are as follows.

Exodus 12:14-20 "This day shall be for you a memorial day, and you shall keep it as a feast to the LORD; throughout your generations, as a statute forever, you shall keep it as a feast. Seven days you shall eat unleavened bread. On the first day you shall remove leaven out of your houses, for if anyone eats what is leavened, from the first day until the seventh day, that person shall be cut off from Israel. On the first day you shall hold a holy assembly, and on the seventh day a holy assembly. No work shall be done on those days. But what everyone needs to eat, that alone may be prepared by you. And you shall observe the Feast of Unleavened Bread, for on this very day I brought your hosts out of the land of Egypt. Therefore you shall observe this day, throughout your generations, as a statute forever. In the first month, from the fourteenth day of the month at evening, you shall eat unleavened bread until the twenty-first day of the month at evening. For seven days no leaven is to be found in your houses. If anyone eats what is leavened, that person will be cut off from the congregation of Israel, whether he is a

sojourner or a native of the land. You shall eat nothing leavened; in all your dwelling places you shall eat unleavened bread."

The focus of the week is to live a life without leaven, the symbol for sin. Leaven is not to be in the house. Leaven products are not to be consumed. Bread without yeast, **matzah**, is to be eaten.

Scripture is clear God's appointed Unleavened Bread took place on the Sabbath.

Luke 23:56 Then they returned and prepared spices and perfumes. And on the Sabbath they rested according to the commandment.

Matthew 27:62-66 Now on the next day, the day after the preparation, the chief priests and the Pharisees gathered together with Pilate, and said, "Sir, we remember that when He was still alive that deceiver said, 'After three days I *am to* rise again.' Therefore, give orders for the grave to be made secure until the third day, otherwise His disciples may come and steal Him away and say to the people, 'He has risen from the dead,' and the last deception will be worse than the first." Pilate said to them, "You have a guard; go, make it *as* secure as you know how." And they went and made the grave secure, and along with the guard they set a seal on the stone.

The religious leaders' actions indicate the days of the week these events took place.

Now on the next day, the day after the preparation... "The next day" is the day after the crucifixion. We know Jesus died on Friday, the day before the current day of the verse. That next day is Saturday or the Sabbath. The Pharisees were concerned with the apostles or followers of Jesus stealing His body. The Pharisees understood Jesus was talking about a resurrection of His dead body. They knew Jesus was calling for a resurrection on the third day, Sunday. The Pharisees wanted a guard at the tomb to stop any hoax. In the end, they provided eyewitnesses and verification of Jesus' resurrection.

Because Unleavened Bread took place on the Sabbath or Saturday, Passover was on Friday. First Fruits was on Sunday.

Leaven is a symbol of sin. Jesus lived a life without sin (leaven).

2 Corinthians 5:21 He made Him who knew no sin to be sin on our behalf, so that we might become the righteousness of God in Him.

Jesus is the unleavened bread.

He is the bread of life.

John 6:35 Jesus said to them, "I am the bread of life; he who comes to Me will not hunger, and he who believes in Me will never thirst.

Jesus was buried and in the grave on the Feast of Unleavened Bread, a Sabbath or Saturday.

Acts 2:19-22 'AND I WILL GRANT WONDERS IN THE SKY ABOVE AND SIGNS ON THE EARTH BELOW, BLOOD, AND FIRE, AND VAPOR OF SMOKE. THE SUN WILL BE TURNED INTO DARKNESS AND THE MOON INTO BLOOD, BEFORE THE GREAT AND GLORIOUS DAY OF THE LORD SHALL COME. AND IT SHALL BE THAT EVERYONE WHO CALLS ON THE NAME OF THE LORD WILL BE SAVED.'

The context of these verses is the day of Pentecost after the death, burial, and resurrection of Christ. Pentecost is 49 days after the First Fruits or the resurrection. It is referred to as Shavuot in the Hebrew. Peter is quoting the prophet **Joel 2:30-32a.**

Acts 2:22 "Men of Israel, listen to these words: Jesus the Nazarene, a man attested to you by God with miracles and wonders and signs which God performed through Him in your midst, just as you yourselves know—

The Apostle Peter brings the definitive hammer when it comes to the timing of the year regarding the death, burial, and resurrection of Jesus Christ. The year is 33 AD.

THE SUN WILL BE TURNED INTO DARKNESS... a solar eclipse.

AND THE MOON INTO BLOOD... a lunar eclipse.

The mathematical work of German Johannes Kepler's allows us to map the exact location of the sun, moon, planets, and stars in time and space. Kepler developed the Laws of Planetary Motion.

THE SUN WILL BE TURNED INTO DARKNESS AND THE MOON INTO BLOOD...

There is only year this could be. There was a solar eclipse on the Jewish New Year, spring equinox, Nisan 1, 33 AD. There was a lunar eclipse, a blood red moon hours after Jesus died on the cross. The moon rose in eclipse as viewed by the people of Jerusalem, Nisan 15, 33 AD.

http://www.bethlehemstar.net/the-day-of-the-cross/peters-argument/

Two Romanian astronomers, Mircea and Oproiu, used a computer program that checked astronomical data against Bible references. Their work confirmed the same date, Nisan 15 (April 3), 33 AD. See link for more detail.

http://www.heraldscotland.com/sport/spl/aberdeen/astronomers-work-out-hour-jesus-died-1.119063

Even NASA, an agency hardly friendly to the Bible, confirms April 3rd in 33 AD with a lunar eclipse viewable in Jerusalem.

http://eclipse.gsfc.nasa.gov/LEhistory/LEhistory.html

Remember, Pilate was in office. Pontius Pilate was the prefect of Judaea from 26 to 36 AD.

Peter is reminding the audience. They **ALL** saw these events. There was no denying it.

Peter saw Jesus walk on water. Peter walked on water himself for a time (**Matthew 14**).

Peter saw Jesus, Moses, and Elijah in glorified bodies at the Transfiguration (**Matthew 17**).

Despite all of these events observed by Peter, the timing of the solar eclipse, and the blood moon, the words of the Bible are more reliable than your senses. It is Peter himself who makes the following statement below in his second epistle.

2 Peter 1:19 *So* **we have the prophetic word** *made* **more sure, to which you do well to pay attention as to a lamp shining in a dark place, until the day dawns and the morning star arises in your hearts.**

First Fruits, Nisan 16, Sunday, 33 AD... The Resurrection

The third of God's holidays is **First Fruits** or **Reshit Katzir** in the Hebrew. The directions for **First Fruits** are noted in **Leviticus 23:9-14.**

Leviticus 23:9-14 And the LORD spoke to Moses, saying, "Speak to the people of Israel and say to them, When you come into the land that I give you and reap its harvest, you shall bring the sheaf of the firstfruits of your harvest to the priest, and he shall wave the sheaf before the LORD, so that you may be accepted. On the day after the Sabbath the priest shall wave it. And on the day when you wave the sheaf, you shall offer a male lamb a year old without blemish as a burnt offering to the LORD. And the grain offering with it shall be two tenths of an ephah of fine flour mixed with oil, a food offering to the LORD with a pleasing aroma, and the drink offering with it shall be of wine, a fourth of a hin. And you shall eat neither bread nor grain parched or fresh until this same day, until you have brought the offering of your God: it is a statute forever throughout your generations in all your dwellings.

The priest is to make a barley offering of the first portion of the harvest to the Lord. The priest intervenes of behalf of the people. The reality of the holiday for the people of Israel is this. The people bring their grain sheaf to the priest. They are to sacrifice a lamb without blemish. The offering is also to be presented with bread and wine.

The holiday begins on the day after the Sabbath or Sunday on our calendar. Jesus was raised on the first day of the week, Sunday.

John 20:1 Now on the first *day* of the week Mary Magdalene came early to the tomb, while it was still dark, and saw the stone *already* taken away from the tomb. See also **Matthew 28:1, Mark 16:1-2,** and **Luke 24:1.**

The gospel accounts confirm the stone had been rolled away and open. The tomb was empty. **Matthew 28:1-8, Mark 16:1-9, Luke 24:1-8.**

Barley is the first grain harvest of the spring harvest. Jesus is the first fruits of the resurrection.

1 Corinthians 15:20-22 But now Christ has been raised from the dead, the first fruits of those who are asleep. For since by a man *came* death, by a man also *came* the resurrection of the dead. For as in Adam all die, so also in Christ all will be made alive.

When looking at a Hebrew calendar, there are four possible years that have the spring holidays in a Friday (Jesus was crucified), Saturday (He was in the grave), Sunday (Christ was resurrected) sequence. These years are 30 AD, 33 AD, 36 AD, and 40 AD.

Luke 3:1 Now in the fifteenth year of the reign of Tiberius Caesar, when Pontius Pilate was governor of Judea, and Herod was tetrarch of Galilee, and his brother <u>Philip</u> was tetrarch of the region of Ituraea and Trachonitis, and Lysanias was tetrarch of Abilene...

The issue is Philip, Herod's brother. Historians have Philip's death at 34 AD. Jesus had to be crucified before 34 AD.

https://sites.google.com/site/calendarstudies/bible-studies/bible_study_year_of_crucifixion

36 AD and 40 AD are omitted. These two possibilities would have the ministry of Jesus longer than 3 to 3 1/2 years as stated in Scripture. The dates would have the ministry lasting 6-10 years or more. These two dates would have Jesus over 40 years old. Jesus was about 30 years old when He started His ministry (**Luke 3:23**).

That leaves 30 AD and 33 AD. Before these dates, Jesus is too young to start His ministry.

The weekend of Nisan 14-16, 33 AD is the only possibility of a blood red lunar eclipse as verified by the Apostle Peter in **Acts 2**. **THE SUN WILL BE TURNED INTO DARKNESS AND THE MOON INTO BLOOD...**

Jesus was resurrected on the Feast of First Fruits, Nisan 16, 33 AD.

Because, He loved us...

Chapter 7 Study Guide

Consider how Jesus relates to the Law during the Passion Week.

What would be the result if Jesus did not fulfil the Law to the letter?

How is Jesus like a Passover Lamb?

It appears, Jesus died on what day of the week?

How many daily sacrifices are there? What were the times of the daily sacrifices? What are the elements?

What time did Jesus' crucifixion begin?

What time did Jesus die?

What natural phenomena occurred during the day of the crucifixion? What year does this point to in recorded history? Name confirming sources of the events?

According to the Law, what time should the Passover Lamb be sacrificed?

How does astronomy potentially confirm the year of Christ's death? What events occurred?

What year does this point towards?

List historical proofs for a 33 AD passion week of Jesus.

Chapter 8

Listen Up!!!

Revelation 3:22 He who has an ear, let him hear what the Spirit says to the churches.

All seven churches in the book of **Revelation** are told... **"He who has an ear, let him hear what the Spirit says to the churches."** This is the last time Jesus addresses the churches. It is an open invitation to whoever wants to listen. We all have ears. Please use them.

Please... "Hear" or **ακουο/akouo**... This is where we get the English word "acoustics". Please listen. Again, the word can mean the following: attend; consider what is or has been said; to understand or perceive the sense of what is said; to find out, learn; to give ear to a teaching or a teacher; to comprehend. Definitions provided by Strong's Concordance.

Seven times, the body of Christ is addressed. Each individual church (Ephesus, Smyrna, Pergamum, Thyatira, Sardis, Philadelphia, and Laodicea) is told. Each single, local church is encouraged to proclaim to the whole body. Please listen.

Revelation 2:7a He who has an ear, let him hear what the Spirit says to the churches...

Revelation 2:11a He who has an ear, let him hear what the Spirit says to the churches...

Revelation 2:17a He who has an ear, let him hear what the Spirit says to the churches...

Revelation 2:29 He who has an ear, let him hear what the Spirit says to the churches.

Revelation 3:6 He who has an ear, let him hear what the Spirit says to the churches.

Revelation 3:13 He who has an ear, let him hear what the Spirit says to the churches.

Revelation 3:22 He who has an ear, let him hear what the Spirit says to the churches.

Please… respond to what the Lord God is saying. There is time now. At some point, conditions are going to deteriorate. God the Father, God the Son, and God the Spirit do not want to crush mankind like a bug. An out into a glorious eternity will be offered. Jesus is not going to give up on people when the going gets tough. He will continue to plea and reach out, even when things turn ugly. The call will be to all of humanity on Earth at this future time.

Revelation 13:9 If anyone has an ear, let him hear:

The next time Christ will make His plea, it will be during the context of the beast or the antichrist. The beast will be physically present on Earth during his reign. In this time, the beast will be in absolute authority, tyranny. The antichrist will demand to be worshipped or one will pay with their earthly, flesh and blood life.

Revelation 13:7-8 Also it was allowed to make war on the saints and to conquer them. And authority was given it over every tribe and people and language and nation, all who dwell on the earth will worship him, everyone whose name has not been written from the foundation of the world in the book of life of the Lamb who has been slain.

The choice for the believer in Jesus will be scary and grim for their present life. The focus will need to be on eternity with God in spite of their earthly circumstances.

Revelation 13:10 If anyone is to be taken captive, to captivity he goes; if anyone is to be slain with the sword, with the sword must he be slain. Here is a call for the endurance and faith of the saints.

Treacherous times are coming. Get over yourself. Don't think you are immune to deception.

Matthew 24:24 For false christs and false prophets will arise and perform great signs and wonders, so as to lead astray, if possible, <u>even the elect</u>.

Matthew 24:25 See, I have told you in advance. -Jesus

Please listen...

Please respond to mercy...

Ephesians 2:4 But God, being rich in mercy, because of the great love with which He loved us...

The Greek word for mercy is **ἔλεος/eleos.** It is defined as pity or compassion. Mercy is being excused from a deserved punishment or outcome. HELPS Word-studies states it is God's loyalty to His covenant. The word is used 27 times in the New Testament.

Eleos is defined as "compassion" in some cases. For example...

Matthew 9:13 Go and learn what this means: 'I desire <u>compassion/mercy</u>, and not sacrifice.' For I came not to call the righteous, but sinners." -Jesus

These are the words of Jesus in **Matthew**. He is quoting **Hosea 6:6.** The issue is one's mental attitude, focus, and heart towards God. The Lord wants our hearts, not acts of religion.

Hosea 6:6 For I desire steadfast love and not sacrifice, the knowledge of God rather than burnt offerings.

The first time "mercy" is used in the Bible is in **Genesis 19:16**. The context is Lot's family and Sodom and Gomorrah. God's action towards Lot and his daughters is "merciful". Notice, Lot and his daughters were spared from the judgment of Sodom and Gomorrah. Lot's wife was extended mercy and she ultimately rejected mercy. Judgment, she became a pillar of salt. It does not matter if one is extended mercy. What are you as an individual going to do with mercy that has been extended to you?

Genesis 19:16 But he lingered. So the men seized him and his wife and his two daughters by the hand, the LORD being <u>merciful</u> to him, and they brought him out and set him outside the city.

This is the Hebrew word **chemlah**. It means pity or compassion just as the Greek word **ἔλεος/eleos**. **Chemlah** comes from the Hebrew word **chamal** which means to spare. The word implies we are responsible. Justice demands judgment. If a transgression is noted, punishment is indicated. The wage of sin is death. But, God is merciful.

Chemlah is used one other time in the Old Testament prophet of **Isaiah**. God is a God of mercy, even in the Old Testament. In the verse below **chemlah** is translated as pity.

Isaiah 63:9 In all their affliction he was afflicted, and the angel of his presence saved them; in his love and in his <u>pity</u> he redeemed them; he lifted them up and carried them all the days of old.

At the time of Isaiah's writing, the verse above had prophetic implications toward the future work of Jesus Christ. Hindsight being 20/20 in the 21st century, we know this is talking about Jesus.

Afflicted... Who took affliction on behalf of an afflicted people?

...the angel of his presence... literally means "messenger of faces". This messenger "saved" or **yasha** in the Hebrew. **Yasha** means to deliver or save from moral trouble. This is the verb form of the root word. The noun form of the word is "Yeshua". Jesus is the English translation of Yeshua. Jesus delivers His people. Yeshua yasha...

God loves us and has compassion towards us. God will send us a "**redeemer**" or **ga`al** in the Hebrew. This is the same word that is used for the kinsman redeemer in the book of **Ruth**. The role of the **ga`al** is to avenge. He will seek revenge on behalf of the people. His blood has paid the ransom for sin. His people will be redeemed from bondage and slavery. Jesus is a kinsman from the tribe of Judah.

The redeemer lifts and bears the responsibility of all the short comings of His people. He is offering if anyone is willing to take the gift.

Please listen, judgment is coming to whole world.

Romans 3:19 Now we know that whatever the law says it speaks to those who are under the law, so that every mouth may be stopped, and the whole world may be held accountable to God.

John 12:31-32 "Now is the judgment of this world; now will the ruler of this world be cast out. And I, when I am lifted up from the earth, will draw all people to myself." -Jesus

Mercy is available. There is time now. Jesus is merciful…

Isaiah 14:26-27 This is the purpose that is purposed concerning the whole earth, and this is the hand that is stretched out over all the nations. For the LORD of hosts has purposed, and who will annul it? His hand is stretched out, and who will turn it back?

Please…

Please respond to grace…

2 Corinthians 12:9 But He said to me, "My grace is sufficient for you, for my power is made perfect in weakness." Therefore I will boast all the more gladly of my weaknesses, so that the power of Christ may rest upon me.

The Greek word for grace is **χάρις/charis.** A form of grace is used 157 times in the New Testament texts. Strong's Concordance defines the word as: as a gift or blessing brought to man by Jesus Christ; favor; gratitude, thanks; a favor, kindness. HELPS Word-studies views the term as the Lord's favor, freely extended to give Himself away to people because He is "always leaning toward them".

Grace is receiving an undeserved gift. None of us truly deserve God's favor. As human beings, we were born in a state of sin. These bodies know nothing but a state of sin. We are not a blank, moral slate born as pure and clean as the wind driven snow. Our sin is not the fault of environmental surroundings. In this life, we are sinners. We should stop blaming others for our short comings. Own it. From our conception, we are ALL under the curse of sin. Always have been, always will be...

Psalm 51:5 Behold, I was brought forth in iniquity, and in sin did my mother conceive me.

Job 1:21 And he said, "Naked I came from my mother's womb, and naked shall I return. The LORD gave, and the LORD has taken away; blessed be the name of the LORD."

Genesis 8:21 And when the LORD smelled the pleasing aroma, the LORD said in his heart, "I will never again curse the ground because of man, for the intention of man's heart is evil from his youth. Neither will I ever again strike down every living creature as I have done.

Psalm 58:3 The wicked are estranged from the womb; they go astray from birth, speaking lies.

None of us are perfect and we all have issues. Some of us out there may think they are flawless or pretty close to it. At the least, they see themselves as better than others. Sorry, there is no sliding scale with sin. The idea that we are all sinners is not a concept noted only in the book of **Romans**. The idea of being sinful humans is noted across the Bible, even in the Old Testament.

Romans 3:10 as it is written: "None is righteous, no, not one..."

Romans 3:23 for all have sinned and fall short of the glory of God...

Psalm 143:2 Enter not into judgment with your servant, for no one living is righteous before you.

Proverbs 20:9 Who can say, "I have made my heart pure; I am clean from my sin"?

Ecclesiastes 7:20 Surely there is not a righteous man on earth who does good and never sins.

1 John 1:8 If we say we have no sin, we deceive ourselves, and the truth is not in us.

In this current state of humanity, we are fallen, imperfect people. Get over your bad self. If we are truly honest with ourselves, deep down, we know we don't cut it with a holy and just God. So... deal with it, we are sinners.

Grace is the operating principle of how God interacts with believers in and through His Son. For those who have not accepted the gracious gift of Jesus Christ, they are still under God's Law regardless of what they believe. Prior to the death, burial, and resurrection of Jesus Christ, humanity was under the Mosaic Law. We are not saved under the Law. The Law points out the fact we are flawed sinners. The standard of the Law defines the fact we are in sin.

John 1:17 For the law was given through Moses; grace and truth came through Jesus Christ.

Romans 6:14 For sin will have no dominion over you, since you are not under law but under grace.

With the cross work of Jesus Christ, things changed. He paid the price for sin. With the cross, there was a new program. And that program is grace. The undeserved gift is eternal life. We don't deserve it. We cannot earn it. The grace of Jesus Christ is a free offering to anyone who will take it. The free gift is grace. Grace and free gift are synonymous.

Romans 5:21 so that, as sin reigned in death, <u>grace</u> also might reign through righteousness leading to eternal life through Jesus Christ our Lord.

Romans 6:23 For the wages of sin is death, but the <u>free gift</u> of God is eternal life in Christ Jesus our Lord.

Romans 6:1 What shall we say then? Are we to continue in sin that grace may abound?

Grace is an interesting and intriguing concept. Grace makes no logical sense. The more one accepts and uses grace, the more grace multiplies and increases. The sting of sin pales in comparison to the power of grace. Sin is no match. Grace wins in a land slide. Accept grace…

Romans 5:20 Now the law came in to increase the trespass, but where sin increased, grace abounded all the more…

1 Timothy 1:14 and the grace of our Lord overflowed for me with the faith and love that are in Christ Jesus.

In **1 Timothy 1**, grace is described as overflowing or **ὑπερπλεονάζω/huperpleonazó.** The prefix "hyper" is used to describe the amount of the number of grace. One cannot measure grace. It is so plentiful, grace cannot be counted. Grace is super, exceedingly abundant. Grace is hyper "cannot be counted". Definition provided by Strong's Concordance.

Grace wins…

Grace is the difference maker, not the individual. We are granted grace by God. It is not about us. Don't get cocky.

Romans 12:3 For by the grace given to me I say to everyone among you not to think of himself more highly than he ought to think, but to think with sober judgment, each according to the measure of faith that God has assigned.

Don't forget, grace is a gift. There is no amount of good deeds or work anyone can do to earn grace. One cannot work for an eternity to earn grace. God is not impressed with your effort. Humble yourself. Get over it because you are not that good. And you are not going to be good enough not matter what you do. Spare God your pride and arrogance. You did not die on a cross to pay for all the sins and transgressions (past, present, and future) of all humanity.

Ephesians 2:8-9 For by grace you have been saved through faith. And this is not your own doing; it is the gift of God, not a result of works, so that no one may boast.

Genesis 6:8 But Noah found <u>favor/grace</u> in the eyes of the LORD.

This is the first mention of the word "grace" in the Bible. This is the Hebrew word **chen**. Sounds like "Cain". Simply put, it is grace or favor. The word is found 69 times in the Old Testament.

God told Noah rain and a flood were coming. Noah was graced with the knowledge of rain and the idea of a flood. The earth had not seen rain prior to Noah.

Genesis 2:5-6 When no bush of the field was yet in the land and no small plant of the field had yet sprung up—for the LORD God had not caused it to rain on the land, and there was no man to work the ground, and a mist was going up from the land and was watering the whole face of the ground...

God gave Noah instructions on how to build a boat.

Genesis 6:14-16 Make yourself an ark of gopher wood. Make rooms in the ark, and cover it inside and out with pitch. This is how you are to make it: the length of the ark 300 cubits, its breadth 50 cubits, and its height 30 cubits. Make a roof for the ark, and finish it to a cubit above, and set the door of the ark in its side. Make it with lower, second, and third decks.

A flood is coming…

Genesis 6:17 For behold, I will bring a flood of waters upon the earth to destroy all flesh in which is the breath of life under heaven. Everything that is on the earth shall die.

God's grace preserved humanity and life through the rain and the flood. Noah and his family lived to tell about it.

Genesis 8:16-17 "Go out from the ark, you and your wife, and your sons and your sons' wives with you. Bring out with you every living thing that is with you of all flesh—birds and animals and every creeping thing that creeps on the earth— that they may swarm on the earth, and be fruitful and multiply on the earth."

If God was not gracious to Noah, we would not be here. Today, in the 21st century, we are benefiting from God's grace in countless ways.

God has been, is, and always will be gracious. The idea that God was not gracious in the Old Testament is absolute nonsense. If God was interested in crushing us like a bug the very moment we sinned, none of us would be here. The population of planet Earth would be zero. The fact we are drawing breath of air is an act of grace.

The notion God is not gracious in the Old Testament is ridiculous. He is not a mean, sadistic God who is looking to squish people with His foot. He has always been gracious. Look at the people who received God's grace in the Old Testament.

Laban recognized God's grace and favor through Jacob.

Genesis 30:27 But Laban said to him, "If I have found <u>favor</u> in your sight, I have learned by divination that the LORD has blessed me because of you."

Joseph was extended grace by God via a prison guard.

Genesis 39:21 But the LORD was with Joseph and showed him steadfast love and gave him <u>favor</u> in the sight of the keeper of the prison.

The nation of Israel was granted favor on the way out of Egypt.

Exodus 11:3 And the LORD gave the people <u>favor</u> in the sight of the Egyptians. Moreover, the man Moses was very great in the land of Egypt, in the sight of Pharaoh's servants and in the sight of the people.

Exodus 12:36 And the LORD had given the people <u>favor</u> in the sight of the Egyptians, so that they let them have what they asked. Thus they plundered the Egyptians.

Moses received God's grace throughout **Exodus 33**. See one of many examples to Moses below.

Exodus 33:12 Moses said to the LORD, "See, you say to me, 'Bring up this people,' but you have not let me know whom you will send with me. Yet you have said, 'I know you by name, and you have also found <u>favor</u> in my sight.'

Gideon received grace and favor from God personally via a sign in **Judges 6:11-27**.

Hannah was granted grace and favor in the birth of Samuel in **1 Samuel 1**.

King David was anointed with grace.

Psalm 45:2 You are the most handsome of the sons of men; <u>grace</u> is poured upon your lips; therefore God has blessed you forever.

Grace is given by God to those who walk in truth.

Psalm 84:11 For the LORD God is a sun and shield; the LORD bestows <u>favor</u> and honor. No good thing does he withhold from those who walk uprightly.

God blesses the afflicted with favor and grace.

Proverbs 3:34 Toward the scorners he is scornful, but to the humble he gives <u>favor</u>.

God's grace for His nation Israel is eternal.

Jeremiah 31:1-3 "At that time, declares the LORD, I will be the God of all the clans of Israel, and they shall be my people." Thus says the LORD: "The people who survived the sword found <u>grace</u> in the wilderness; when Israel sought for rest, the LORD appeared to him from far away. I have loved you with an everlasting love; therefore I have continued my faithfulness to you..."

God's Grace is better than material wealth despite what the culture says.

Proverbs 22:1 A good name is to be chosen rather than great riches, and <u>favor</u> is better than silver or gold.

And yes, God's grace in Jesus Christ is promised from the Old Testament prophet **Zechariah**.

Zechariah 12:10 "And I will pour out on the house of David and the inhabitants of Jerusalem a spirit of <u>grace</u> and pleas for mercy, so that, when they look on me, on him whom they have pierced, they shall mourn for him, as one mourns for an only child, and weep bitterly over him, as one weeps over a firstborn..."

Acts 2:38 And Peter said to them, "Repent and be baptized every one of you in the name of Jesus Christ for the <u>forgiveness</u> of your sins, and you will receive the gift of the Holy Spirit.

ἄφεσις /aphesis is the Greek word for "forgiveness". The term is used 19 times in the New Testament. The word is defined as: a sending away, a letting go, a release, pardon, complete forgiveness, remission, or deliverance. "Forgiveness" is releasing someone from obligation or debt. This is a legal term.

"Forgiveness" is primarily used in relation to the debt of sin in the New Testament. The obligation of sin is death.

Romans 6:23 For the wages of sin is death, but the free gift of God is eternal life in Christ Jesus our Lord.

Ezekiel 18:4 Behold, all souls are Mine; the soul of the father as well as the soul of the son is Mine. The soul who sins will die.

The primary word in the Hebrew regarding "forgiveness" is **salach**. The word is used 47 times in the Old Testament. It means to forgive or pardon. **Salach** is the word used in relation to God's forgiveness in the Hebrew texts. Definitions provided by Strong's Concordance.

Despite what the critic may say, "forgiveness" is built into the Mosaic Law. God has always been forgiving. God extends "forgiveness" to the individual as well as the nation of Israel. Below are a couple of many examples.

God is not a male chauvinist pig. God stands up for women's rights. He forgives women and girls even when opposed by men or fathers. In fact, this is the first time the word "forgiveness" or **salach** is used in the Bible. God's first example of "forgiveness" is granted to a female in regards to an overbearing father.

Numbers 30:5 But if her father opposes her on the day that he hears of it, no vow of hers, no pledge by which she has bound herself shall stand. And the LORD <u>will forgive</u> her, because her father opposed her.

The high priest made a sacrifice to the Lord on behalf of the nation Israel for sin. As a thought, do we have a high priest who sacrificed Himself on behalf of His people?

Numbers 15:25 And the priest shall make atonement for all the congregation of the people of Israel, and they <u>shall be forgiven</u>, because it was a mistake, and they have brought their offering, a food offering to the LORD, and their sin offering before the LORD for their mistake.

The new covenant in the forgiveness of sins is promised from the Old Testament prophet of **Jeremiah**. Jesus Himself confirmed this "new covenant" in the upper room with His disciples.

Luke 22:20 And likewise the cup after they had eaten, saying, "This cup that is poured out for you is the new covenant in my blood." -Jesus

The forgiveness of the "new covenant" is quoted completely in **Hebrews 8:8-12.**

Jeremiah 31:31-34 "Behold, the days are coming, declares the LORD, when I will make a new covenant with the house of Israel and the house of Judah, not like the covenant that I made with their fathers on the day when I took them by the hand to bring them out of the land of Egypt, my covenant that they broke, though I was their husband, declares the LORD. For this is the covenant that I will make with the house of Israel after those days, declares the LORD: I will put my law within them, and I will write it on their hearts. And I will be their God, and they shall be my people. And no longer shall each one teach his neighbor and each his brother, saying, 'Know the LORD,' for they shall all know me, from the least of them to the greatest, declares the LORD. For I <u>will forgive</u> their iniquity, and I will remember their sin no more."

Multiple people bear witness to the fact, Jesus Christ is the Lamb of God. The first example is a quote from John the Baptist in the Book of **John**. The identification of Christ as the Lamb of God took place in the Jordan River at the baptism of Jesus.

John 1:29 The next day he saw Jesus coming toward him, and said, "Behold, the Lamb of God, who takes away the sin of the world!"

A day later, John the Baptist again identified Jesus as the Lamb of God.

John 1:36 and he looked at Jesus as he walked by and said, "Behold, the Lamb of God!"

While Philip was with the Ethiopian, he equated Jesus as the referenced lamb from the reading of **Isaiah 53:7.**

Acts 8:32 Now the passage of the Scripture that he was reading was this: "Like a sheep he was led to the slaughter and like a lamb before its shearer is silent, so he opens not his mouth."

The Apostle Peter states the blood of Jesus is as a sinless lamb.

1 Peter 1:19 but with precious blood, as of a lamb unblemished and spotless, the blood of Christ.

In these four cases above, Jesus is referred to as an ἀμνός/amnos in the Greek. A lamb with innocence and sacrificial considerations is the idea per Strong's Concordance.

In the book of **Revelation**, John refers to Jesus as a lamb or ἀρνίον/arnion. This is a small, little, or diminutive lamb. This type of person has the purest of intentions. HELPs Word Studies indicates the essence of innocence or virgin like intentions. Twenty-nine times (29) Christ is labeled as an **"arnion"** only in the book of **Revelation**. The context is the throne room of Heaven in the presence of the Father, Spirit, millions of witnesses including apostles, elders, believers, martyrs, creatures, and angels.

It is "the" Lamb. There is a Greek definite article in front of "Lamb". The text literally reads... "the lamb" in the original Greek. Jesus Christ is "the" Lamb.

Revelation 5:12 saying with a loud voice, "Worthy is the Lamb who was slain, to receive power and wealth and wisdom and might and honor and glory and blessing!"

Revelation 14:1 Then I looked, and behold, on Mount Zion stood the Lamb, and with Him 144,000 who had His name and His Father's name written on their foreheads.

Revelation 17:14 They will make war on the Lamb, and the Lamb will conquer them, for He is Lord of lords and King of kings, and those with Him are called and chosen and faithful.

Jesus Christ is the sacrificial Lamb of God's Appointed Spring Feasts.

The lamb is **without blemish** or "tamim" in the Hebrew. The lamb is complete or sound per Strong's Concordance.

Exodus 12:5-6 Your <u>lamb</u> shall be without blemish, a male a year old. You may take it from the sheep or from the goats, and you shall keep it until the fourteenth day of this month, when the whole assembly of the congregation of Israel shall kill their lambs at twilight.

Jesus Christ is the sacrificial Lamb of God's Appointed Spring Feasts. A "pesach" is an unblemished lamb which was required for the sacrifice. Christ is the "pesach".

Jesus Christ is the sacrificial Lamb of God as foreshadowed by Moses in **Exodus 12**.

Please, turn and respond to the Lamb...

Judgment is coming. The seven-year period of tribulation will be marked by spiritual deception, world war, economic upheaval, famine, disease, asteroids, extreme weather, and on and on and on...

Jesus said it best.

Matthew 24:21-22 For then there will be great tribulation, such as has not been from the beginning of the world until now, no, and never will be. And if those days had not been cut short, no human being would be saved. But for the sake of the elect those days will be cut short.

Revelation 6:12 I looked when He broke the sixth seal, and there was a great earthquake; and the sun became black as sackcloth *made* of hair, and the whole moon became like blood...

The context of the set of verses in **Revelation 6** is the initial third of the Tribulation, the seals. This event takes place approximately 7 years before the beginning of Christ's Kingdom. Granted, there appears to be significant issues with the sun, moon, stars, atmosphere and sky in this context. But, the focus of the section is the geological and geographical changes coming to planet Earth.

The earthquake starts the chain of events in the sixth seal. The quake is described as "great" or μεγασ /megas in the Greek. It can be translated as significant, severe, gigantic, or YUGE (huge) per Strong's Concordance. This earthquake will be a big deal.

Revelation 6:14 The sky was split apart like a scroll when it is rolled up, and every mountain and island were moved out of their places.

...and every mountain and island were moved out of their places... This is exactly what the verse says in the Greek. "Every" mountain and island will be moved out of its place. Each, every, the whole, all of them are moved.

The root word for "moved" is **κινεο/kineo**. It can also be translated: to cause to go, to move, set in motion. Figuratively, it will cause a commotion (NET Bible/Strong's Concordance).

This verse is suggesting tectonic plate movement and change across the planet. The earthquake will knock things out of their place. Consider all of the mountain ranges in the world: The Rockies, Andes, Urals, Alps, Himalayas... Consider all of the islands in the world...

Recent history has not seen an earthquake that has caused continents to initiate movement and drifting. Modern day maps and globes will be obsolete.

Revelation 6:15 Then the kings of the earth and the great men and the commanders and the rich and the strong and every slave and free man hid themselves in the caves and among the rocks of the mountains;

God does not care how deep your bunker is. God does not care how much you have prepared. God does not care if you are the leader of a country. Military training will not save you. He does not care how much money and wealth one has acquired. Your intellect is no match for the Lamb, Jesus. It does not matter if you are isolated. A piece of advice to the social elite, you can run but you cannot hide.

Revelation 6:16 and they said to the mountains and to the rocks, "Fall on us and hide us from the presence of Him who sits on the throne, and from the wrath of the Lamb..."

Be careful what you wish for. God will give you what you want. **Revelation 16:20** beckons.

Revelation 8:5 Then the angel took the censer and filled it with the fire of the altar, and threw it to the earth; and there followed peals of thunder and sounds and flashes of lightning and an <u>earthquake</u>.

Revelation 11:13 And in that hour there was a great <u>earthquake</u>, and a tenth of the city fell; seven thousand people were killed in the <u>earthquake</u>, and the rest were terrified and gave glory to the God of heaven.

Revelation 11:19 And the temple of God which is in heaven was opened; and the ark of His covenant appeared in His temple, and there were flashes of lightning and sounds and peals of thunder and an <u>earthquake</u> and a great hailstorm.

Revelation 16:18 And there were flashes of lightning and sounds and peals of thunder; and there was a great <u>earthquake</u>, such as there had not been since man came to be upon the earth, so great an <u>earthquake</u> *was it, and* so mighty.

This set of quakes takes place seven years before the Millennial Kingdom. Geography and geology are going to change for planet Earth. Each earthquake will increase with regard to intensity. The first quake in **Revelation 6:12** moves mountains and islands out of their place. A seismic chain of reaction is started. Additional quakes will facilitate further land mass movement. The land we live on floats on molten lava and magma. The last quake in **Revelation 16:18** will be the greatest in the history of man.

A pattern emerges with earthquakes in the book of **Revelation**. Earthquakes mark the end of each set of judgments (seals, trumpets, and bowls). The first earthquake in **Revelation 6:12** is the sixth seal. The quake in **Revelation 8:5** occurs before the beginning of the trumpet judgments. It is the seventh seal. The earthquake in **Revelation 11:13** marks the sixth trumpet of seven. The quake in **Revelation 11:19** is the seventh trumpet before the bowl judgments. The last earthquake in **Revelation 16:18** marks the end of the seven bowl judgments.

In addition to the quake activity, imagine the collateral events associated. It is plausible to imagine significant volcanic eruptions which spew dust, ash, steam, and gases into the atmosphere. Tsunamis are highly likely. Breathing is going to be difficult.

Joel 2:30-31 I will display wonders in the sky and on the earth, blood, fire and columns of smoke. The sun will be turned into darkness and the moon into blood before the great and awesome day of the LORD comes.

Revelation 11:13... Jerusalem is the city referenced. Today in 2019, Jerusalem's population is estimated to be around 919,000+. The verse states a tenth of city's infrastructure is destroyed. 7,000 people are prophesied to die in this earthquake.

This earthquake is also the exclamation point for the resurrection of the two witnesses of **Revelation 11**. People refuse to bury these two guys after they are killed by the antichrist. They are left to rot as an example. The citizens of Earth are throwing a party in honor of their death.

https://paulthepoke.com/2015/01/18/antichrist-the-beast-part-1/

<u>The Revelation Record</u> by Dr. Henry M. Morris; Tyndale House Publishers, Wheaton, IL; Creation-Life Publishers, San Diego, CA, 1983.

Revelation 16:17-20 The seventh angel poured out his bowl into the air, and a loud voice came out of the temple, from the throne, saying, "It is done!" And there were flashes of lightning, rumblings, peals of thunder, and a great earthquake such as there had never been since man was on the earth, so great was that earthquake. The great city was split into three parts, and the cities of the nations fell, and God remembered Babylon the great, to make her drain the cup of the wine of the fury of his wrath. And every island fled away, and no mountains were to be found.

The context of this verse is before the Second Coming of Christ. It occurs near the end of the seven-year Tribulation. The Millennial Kingdom is about to commence. The seventh bowl concludes the judgments upon the earth and humanity.

...and a great earthquake such as there had never been since man was on the earth, so great was that earthquake. The last earthquake mentioned in the Bible will be the largest and strongest in the history of humanity. This earthquake will also be the most destructive. The Greek expression of the quake is restated three times. The earthquake is greatness and magnitude upon greatness and magnitude upon greatness and magnitude. The scale and power are larger than the Discovery Channel can imagine. It is the Mega Quake!

The great city was split into three parts. The great city is mystery Babylon. Some think the city is a reborn Babylon in modern day Iraq. Others think it is Rome, Italy. Some believe it is Istanbul, Turkey. Mecca, Saudi Arabia is a city on seven hills. Pick your seven hilled city. Conjecture in regards to the city is fun but does not matter in the grand scheme of things.

...and the cities of the nations fell... All the cities (plural) of the nations (plural) are doomed. The Greek word for "fell" is πιπτο/**pipto**. Per Strong's Concordance, it means: to descend from a higher place to a lower; to be thrust down; come to an end, disappear, cease; to lose authority, no longer have force. Metaphorically: to fall under judgment, came under condemnation. **"It is done!"**

And every island fled away, and no mountains were to be found. The idea of no more mountains and changed geography is noted in multiple places in the Bible. **Revelation** is not the only source of this concept.

Psalm 97:5 The mountains melt like wax before the LORD, before the Lord of all the earth.

Psalm 46:6 The nations rage, the kingdoms totter; he utters his voice, the earth melts.

Isaiah 24:1 Behold, the LORD lays the earth waste, devastates it, distorts its surface and scatters its inhabitants.

Isaiah 24:19 The earth is utterly broken, the earth is split apart, the earth is violently shaken.

Micah 1:4 And the mountains will melt under him, and the valleys will split open, like wax before the fire, like waters poured down a steep place.

The level of destruction is unimaginable. We cannot comprehend. It says what it says.

Genesis 49:8-10 Judah, your brothers shall praise you; your hand shall be on the neck of your enemies; your father's sons shall bow down before you. Judah is a lion's cub; from the prey, my son, you have gone up. He stooped down; he crouched as a lion and as a lioness; who dares rouse him? The scepter shall not depart from Judah, nor the ruler's staff from between his feet, until Shiloh comes; and to him shall be the obedience of the peoples.

The promise of the Jewish Messiah coming from the line of Judah has its foundation in **Genesis 49**. Israel or Jacob is on his death bed. His sons have been called and prophetic blessing is being announced. The focus is on the line of Judah.

Judah means "praised" in the Hebrew.

Judah's family line was chosen by God because of His grace. Judah was far from perfect. He was greedy in dealing his brother Joseph (**Genesis 37:26**). Judah committed adultery with a prostitute. The result was a child. (**Genesis 38:18**).

Genesis 49:8a Judah, your brothers shall praise you; your hand shall be on the neck of your enemies; your father's sons shall bow down before you. Judah was granted the birthright leadership position in the family as if he was the first born. Future leadership was to descend from the line of Judah. He was promised to be successful in matters of war and conflict.

Genesis 49:9a Judah is a lion's cub; from the prey... This is how the line of Judah started in King David. He was the little runt who challenged the giant Goliath. Like a lion's **"cub"** or **"whelp"**, David was a kid when he approached battle. David was portrayed as overmatched **"prey"** against the giant Philistine. All he had was a sling and five rocks.

Genesis 49:9b ...he crouched as a lion and as a lioness; who dares rouse him? At some point, a future Messiah from the line of David will be stretched out, relaxed, comfortable, and in absolute control. He will be firmly established. Nobody will dare challenge Him.

Genesis 49:10a The scepter shall not depart from Judah... This was not fulfilled until King David 1,000 years before Jesus Christ. From the time of King David until the time of Christ, a king from the line of Judah ruled. There has been a gap of almost 2,000 years since the Jewish people were scattered from Israel in 70 AD. King David was the first in the line of Judah. There will be another and He will be the last.

Genesis 49:10b ...nor the ruler's staff from between his feet... Some scholars take this phrase to be idiomatic language in reference to the genitals. Descendants are to come from "**between his feet**" is the idea. And these descendants are to be rulers.

Genesis 49:10c ...until Shiloh comes... The definitive meaning of **Shiloh** is not clear. Strong's Concordance defines the term as: he whose it is; that which belongs to him; tranquility. Ancient Jews took the term "**Shiloh**" to mean the Messiah.

Genesis 49:10d ...and to him shall be the obedience of the peoples. The idea in the Hebrew is the nations will be cleansed and purged. The Messiah is going to clean house.

Revelation 5:5 And one of the elders said to me, "Weep no more; behold, the Lion of the tribe of Judah, the Root of David, has conquered, so that He can open the scroll and its seven seals."

John identifies **the Lion of the tribe of Judah** as Jesus Christ.

The Lamb of God is currently at the right hand of the Father in Heaven. And when He returns to Earth, He will rule and reign with a rod of iron as **the Lion of the Tribe of Judah.**

There is time now. Identify with the sinless Lamb of God who takes away the sin of the world.

Please...

Please...

Please...

Chapter 8 Study Guide

Define "hear" or **ακουο/akouo.** As a body of Christ, are we "hearing"? Individually, are we "hearing"? Discuss.

Define "mercy" and "grace". Are the terms different in meaning? If different, how so?

Give examples of "mercy" and "grace" from the Bible and in your life.

What is the point and purpose of the Mosaic Law?

How does God's "grace" work? How much "grace" is there?

What have you done to earn God's "grace"? If you have listed one or more deeds or works, repeat Chapter 3 regarding The Gospel.

List examples of God's "grace" towards Noah.

List of examples of God's "grace" in the Old Testament.

Define "forgiveness".

Describe and discuss the first time God demonstrates "forgiveness" in the Bible.

Where in the Bible is the promise of the new covenant in the forgiveness of sins? Analyze and discuss.

List examples of who identifies the Lamb of God. Who is the Lamb of God?

What is the significance of the sacrificial lamb as it relates to the Mosaic Law?

Describe the scope and scale of the earthquake mentioned in **Revelation 6**.

Describe and discuss the progression of earthquakes throughout the course of **Revelation**.

Describe and discuss the last earthquake mention in the Bible in **Revelation 16**.

Who is the Lion of the tribe of Judah? Where is the prophecy of His promised coming?

Who was the first king from the Tribe of Judah? Who will be the last king from the Tribe of Judah?

Thanks for taking the time to purchase and read the book. If you enjoyed the book, please take the time to review at your favorite retailer.

Thanks, Paul

About the Author

Paul Lehr is a Speech Pathologist and home health provider. The majority of his work focuses on swallowing disorders in neurologically impaired patients. He has been a business owner for the past 20 plus years. Paul earned his BS in Speech Pathology and Audiology from Oklahoma State University. His MA was completed in Speech Pathology at Oklahoma State University.

When Paul's son was born prematurely in 2003, there was lots of support from family and friends. Keeping up with phone calls was too much. So, he provided e-mails with updates on health and well-being. In time, his son was healthy and came home. The e-mails stopped but Paul was encouraged to keep writing.

Three years later, Paul was asked to assist in writing a Sunday school curriculum. The lessons were well received by the local body and on the church website. Again, he was encouraged to keep writing. Next, Paul taught a Sunday School class for junior high and high school students. He would share notes with others from the class he was teaching.

Later, a young man at a local church encouraged Paul to start a blog. The website focuses on topical studies such as the Gospel of Jesus Christ, creation, God's Appointed Holidays and Feasts, end times prophecy, ancient Hebrew cultural customs, the Prophet Isaiah, and various topical studies. Three years later, Paul's son told him, "Dad, you need to do updates on how the news is tied to the Bible." The "Trend Update" was born.

A friend and fellow Boy Scout father encouraged Paul to start a YouTube channel along with other social media outlets.

Years later, God's prophetic words have reached tens of millions in over 190 countries.

Isaiah 55:11 So will My word be which goes forth from My mouth; it will not return to Me empty, without accomplishing what I desire, and without succeeding in the matter for which I sent it.

That same Boy Scout father would later introduce Paul to the documentaries of Trey Smith and the God in a Nutshell Project. Paul is the editor and a featured author on the God in a Nutshell website and project.

Guest speak and presenter duties have focused on the topics of the Gospel of Jesus Christ in God's Appointed Spring Feasts and current events related to Bible prophecy.

At this time, Paul would like to encourage each individual to learn about who God is. Because one way or another, we are all eternal. The issue is our destiny.

Connect with Me on Social Media

Website: https://paulthepoke.com/

Twitter: @PaulthePoke

Facebook: https://www.facebook.com/PaulLLehr/

Author: https://godinanutshell.com/

Book Cover by God in a Nutshell Project, Laura Winkler

Photo: Stephanie Weismann, Life Touch

www.ingramcontent.com/pod-product-compliance
Lightning Source LLC
Chambersburg PA
CBHW031455040426
42444CB00007B/1111